T0362958

PUBLISHED BY BOOM BOOKS
boombooks.biz

ABOUT THIS SERIES

.... But after that, I realised that I knew very little about these parents of mine. They had been born about the start of the Twentieth Century, and they died in 1970 and 1980. For their last 50 years, I was old enough to speak with a bit of sense.

I could have talked to them a lot about their lives. I could have found out about the times they lived in. But I did not. I know almost nothing about them really. Their courtship? Working in the pits? The Lock-out in the Depression? Losing their second child? Being dusted as a miner? The shootings at Rothbury? My uncles killed in the War? Love on the dole? There were hundreds, thousands of questions that I would now like to ask them. But, alas, I can't. It's too late.

Thus, prompted by my guilt, I resolved to write these books. They describe happenings that affected people, real people. The whole series is, to coin a modern phrase, designed to push your buttons, to make you remember and wonder at things forgotten. The books might just let nostalgia see the light of day, so that oldies and youngies will talk about the past and re-discover a heritage otherwise forgotten. Hopefully, they will spark discussions between generations, and foster the asking and answering of questions that should not remain unanswered.

BORN IN 1963?

WHAT ELSE HAPPENED?

RON WILLIAMS

AUSTRALIAN SOCIAL HISTORY

BOOK 25 IN A SERIES OF 35

FROM 1939 to 1973

War Babies Years (1939 to 1945): 7 Titles

Baby Boom Years (1946 to 1960): 15 Titles

Post Boom Years (1961 to 1970): 13 Titles

BOOM, BOOM BABY, BOOM

BORN IN 1963? WHAT ELSE HAPPENED?

Published by Boom Book
Wickham, NSW, Australia
Web: www.boombooks.biz
Email: jen@boombooks.biz

Creator: Williams, Ron, 1934- author.
Title: Born in 1963? : what else happened? / Ron Williams.
ISBN: 9780648651161
Australia--Social conditions--20th century.

Cover images: National Archives of Australia A1200, L44666 Prime Minister Robert Menzies; A1200, L44010 Family group at the Easter Show; A1200, L42988 Dr Tatiana Jelihovsky, cancer research fellowship winner; A1200, L44032 Boomerang instructions.

TABLE OF CONTENTS

IMPORTANT FACTS

PRIME MINISTER: BOB MENZIES

DEPUTY PRIME MINISTER: HAROLD HOLT

LEADER OF OPPOSITION: ARTHUR CALWELL

DEPUTY LEADER: GOUGH WHITLAM

MONARCH: QUEEN ELIZABETH II

CONSORT: PRINCE PHILLIP

BRITISH PRIME MINISTER: HAROLD McAMILLAN

NEW PRIME MINISTER: ALEC DOUGLAS-HOME

 PRESIDENT OF USA: JOHN KENNEDY

NEW PRESIDENT: LYNDON JOHNSTON

POPE: JOHN XXIII

NEW POPE: JOHN PAUL II

MELBOURNE CUP: 1962: EVEN STEVENS

MELBOURNE CUP: 1963: GATUM GATUM

MELBOURNE CUP: 1964: POLO PRINCE

TOP SELLING MOVIE: CLEOPATRA

BEST PICTURE: TOM JONES

BEST ACTOR: SIDNEY POITIER

BEST ACTRESS: PATRICIA NEAL

PREFACE TO THIS SERIES: 1939 TO 1973

This book is the 25th in a series of books that I aim to publish. It tells a story about a number of important or newsworthy events that happened in 1963. The series will cover each of the years from 1939 to 1970, for a total of thirty-two books, which should just about bring me to the end of my thoroughly undistinguished writing career.

I developed my interest in writing these books a few years ago at a time when my children entered their teens. My own teens started in 1947, and I started trying to remember what had happened to me then. I thought of the big events first, like Saturday afternoon at the pictures, and cricket in the back yard, and the wonderful fun of going to Maitland on the train for school each day. Then I recalled some of the not-so-good things. I was an altar boy, and that meant three or four Masses a week. I might have thought I loved God at that stage, but I really hated his Masses. And the schoolboy bullies, like Greg Farrell, and the hapless Freddie Evans. Yet, to compensate for these, there was always the beautiful, black headed, blue-sailor-suited June Brown, who I was allowed to worship from a distance.

I also thought about my parents. Most of the major events that I lived through came to mind readily. But after that, I realised that I really knew very little about these parents of mine. They had been born about the start of the Twentieth Century, and they died in 1970 and 1980. For their last 20 years, I was old enough to speak with a bit of sense. I could have talked to them a lot about their lives. I could have found out about the times they lived in. But I did not. I know almost nothing about them really. Their courtship? Working in the pits? The Lock-out in the Depression? Losing their second child? Being dusted as a miner? The shootings at Rothbury? My uncles killed in the War? There were hundreds, thousands of questions that I would now like to ask them. But, alas, I can't. It's too late.

Thus, prompted by my guilt, I resolved to write these books. They describe happenings that affected people, real people. In every year, there is some coverage of international affairs, but a lot more on housing, politics, delinquency, doctors, larrikins, and dogs. The whole series is, to coin a modern phrase, designed to push the reader's buttons, to make you remember and wonder at things forgotten. The books might just let nostalgia see the light of day, so that oldies and youngies will talk about the past and re-discover a heritage otherwise forgotten. Hopefully, they will spark discussions between generations, and foster the asking and the answering of questions that should not remain unanswered.

The sources of my material. I was born in 1934, so that I can remember well a great deal of what went on around me from 1946 onwards. But of course, the bulk of this book's material came from research. That meant that I spent many hours on-line at home, and at various public libraries reading microfilms of newspapers, magazines, periodicals and so on. My task here was to sift out day-by-day those stories and events that would be of interest to the most readers. Then I supplemented these with materials from books, broadcasts, memoirs, biographies, government reports and statistics, Ministers' statements, and the like. And I talked to old-timers, one-on-one, and in organised groups, and to Baby Boomers about their recollections. People with stories to tell come out of the woodwork, and talk no end about the tragic and funny and commonplace events that have shaped their lives.

The presentation of each book. For each year covered, the end result is a collection of short Chapters on many of the topics that concerned ordinary people in that year. I think I have covered most of the major issues that people then were interested in. On the other hand, in some cases I have dwelt a little on minor frivolous matters, perhaps to the detriment of more sober considerations. Still, in the long run, this makes the book more readable, and hopefully it will convey adequately the spirit of the times.

Each of the books is mainly Sydney based, but **I have been deliberately national in outlook**, so that readers elsewhere will feel comfortable that I am talking about matters that affected them personally. After all, housing shortages and strikes and a tuberculosis epidemic involved all Australians, and other issues, such as problems overseas, had no State component in them. Overall, I expect I can make you wonder, remember, rage and giggle equally, no matter where you hail from.

NEWS OF THE WORLD

Throughout 1963, there was always a ton of news coming from the propaganda machines on our side of the Cold War. You will remember that the US and Russia were locked in a deadly struggle to convince the rest of the world that one of them was the goodie, and the other one was a baddie, and they were prepared to do all sorts of things to get that result, provided that they were not caught out. It was an apparently endless struggle that had been going on for a decade, and would go on for three more.

We in Australia were firmly committed to the American cause. So we got all their news reports, all of their free propaganda

TV and radio reports, the visits from their fleets, their movies and songs, their way of dress, their cars and what have you. Much of this was good fun and we welcomed it all.

But some of it, I believe, was dead boring. In particular, the reports about their dealings with the Reds in Russia and China and elsewhere. Every day in the newspapers there were half a dozen reports or references to how the Yanks were trying to solve the world's problems, and how the Reds were doing their best to thwart the Yanks. Whether it was tariffs, boundaries, nuclear behavior, alliance between countries, refugees, uprisings of native populations, gifts of armaments, spies, or diplomatic relationships, the two super-powers were at loggerheads. And always talking tough.

I have adopted the policy in this book of not reporting much of these activities. Where something merits inclusion, I have reported it. Otherwise, I advise you now to keep somewhere in the back of your mind that the Cold War was still a reality, that all the connivings I just mentioned were still going on, and that there were some persons in Australia, other than myself, who took them seriously. But not me.

While I am at it, I will also say I take the same attitude to strikes here in Oz. There were lots of them, and the wharfies were the current main villains. But they came and went. The Reds were always found guilty, and so they should have been, though in some cases the strikers did have a real grievance against the bosses. Be that as it may, except for the occasional reference, I will just assume that you will remember that **strikes were a constant feature of life in 1963**, and that you do not need a blow-by-blow coverage of these in my limited pages.

OUR TRADE POSITION

For most of the years from Federation, Australia had traded as a most favoured nation with Britain. That means we had long term contracts with the Brits that served the purposes of both nations.

It helped the Brits because they did not have to shop around all over the worlds for their basic agricultural products with constantly changing prices and dubious deliveries.

It helped us because our farmers and graziers and growers could plan ahead, reasonably confident that if they could produce a certain amount, they would be able to sell it. A nice comfortable situation that was rare in world terms of trade.

Now, however, Britain was talking more and more, and acting more and more, about joining a Common Market with Europe. No one was at all certain about what this would mean for Oz, but it was certain that the existing trade preference deals with the Brits would end.

This was starting to send shivers up the backs of our politicians and our agricultural interests. They would need to find markets somewhere in the world, but where? Under what terms and conditions? After so many years of not marketing world-wide, could we now suddenly learn to do this? Questions were growing faster than the crops.

So, for the nation that had ridden on the sheep's back for so long, this problem was lurking. 1963 was the year when it became so obvious that people actually started talking about it and what effect it would have.

MY RULES IN WRITING

Now we are just about ready to go. First, though, I give you a few Rules I follow as I write. They will help you understand where I am coming from.

Note. Throughout this book, I rely a lot on reproducing **Letters from the newspapers.** Whenever I do this, I put the text in a different font, and indent it a little, and make the font somewhat smaller. **I do not edit the text at all. The same is true for the** *News Items* **at the start of each Chapter.** That is, I do not correct spelling or grammar, and if the text gets at all garbled, I do not correct it. It's just as it was seen in the Papers.

Second Note. The **material** for this book, when it comes from newspapers, is reported as it was seen at the time. If the benefit of hindsight over the years changes things, then I might record that in my Comments. **The info reported thus reflects matters as they were seen in 1963**

Third Note. Let me also apologise in advance to anyone I might offend. In a work such as this, it is certain some people will think **I got some things wrong. I am sure that I did**, but please remember, all of this is only my opinion. And really, **my opinion does not matter one little bit in the scheme of things. I hope you will say "silly old bugger", and shrug your shoulders, and read on.**

OFF WE GO

So now we are ready to plunge into 1963. Let's go, and I trust you will have a pleasant trip.

JANUARY NEWS ITEMS

The polio disease had been plaguing Australia for the last decade. **In 1962, new Sabin and Salk vaccines became available**, and wide-spread inoculations were done on the vulnerable. As a result, Health Department announced that **polio rates had fallen by 97 per cent in the last six months.**

The European Common Market now had six members. These were West Germany, France, Holland, Belgium, Denmark and Italy. **For the last ten years**, the Brits had been talking, on and off, about joining up with these nations, and **might** now be ready to do so. But it was not as simple as that. France in mid-January stated that **the Brits were not welcome**, and that it was ready to veto their entry….

If Britain entered, **Australia would lose many trade advantages it enjoyed** with the Brits. Many people in Oz argued that **we wanted Britain to stay out**, and thus avoid the problem of finding new markets. It was pretty comfortable here now. So, on the surface, the French President de Gaulle's stance was welcomed here.

The **Basic Wage** was paid to employees at the bottom end of the wages scale. It was designed to be the minimum amount that **a man with a wife and two children needed in order to live....**

Under the social conditions of the day, in 1963, **the rate was higher for men because the man was the bread-winner for the entire family.**

1963: HERE WE COME

For me, as a writer, January comes at the right time each year. I say this because for most of the month, the population of Australia is in holiday mode. That means that just about everyone has packed up and moved to somewhere else. Country people come to the seaside, and city people go to the bush. They move into flats and units and shacks and tents and lodgings and caravans, and forget about all the things that worry them for the rest of the year. Business stands still, bread is generally staler, trains are always crowded, the beaches are full, and the newspapers are only half size.

It is because of these **newspapers** that I say that January comes at the right time. Right across this wonderful land of Oz, our **newspapers are very different at this time**. Normally, they have worked hard at catching readers' attention with an endless stream of stories about terrible events that had just happened, or hopefully might soon. There was always something that could cause worries, outrages that had happened to others and maybe would come to you, inequities and bad decisions from bureaucrats, local Councils who got everything wrong, and of course, the buffoons in State and Federal governments. This was the normal readers' fare for eleven months of the year, and generally he could find something in the mix to keep his interest.

Every January, it was all different. The newspapers dropped or minimised there terrible stories from overseas, and their worrisome forecasts for us locally. The journalists were enjoying a few weeks off, and all levels of Government were also on holidays, so there was no point in complaining about their outrages. It made for a nice serene setting, where news from the outside world scarcely penetrated into the holiday cocoon, and the cricket and the tennis became a national obsession. The whole nation was in holiday mode, and wanted no part of the real world that had just about exhausted them in the eleven months up to Christmas.

This is always good for me. January is the month when new readers of my books, such as yourselves, need to be introduced to past and ongoing events, and the characters who are making the news. The quiet month of January is the ideal time to do this, because so little other news is coming through. Of course, there are the perennial stories about how bad the Russians and Chinese are, and about how the world should be lying awake all night listening for a atomic explosion, and how terrible it is in some African nation with the natives all rising up and wanting independence. Of course, such stories had their elements of truth in them, but **this month,** to most Aussies, they meant nothing. But for me, their absence gives me the chance to introduce the stories in my book.

This January was an exception to this pattern. A most spectacular exception indeed, because of the very intriguing **Bogle and Chandler** story. I will come back to **that** in a few pages, but right now I will take the opportunity to introduce three topics that are currently already in the news.

THREE ON-GOING MATTERS

The first of these concerns this nation's attitude to Red China. This relatively new Communist State was at loggerheads with the USA, and that meant that we – Australia - were decidedly unfriendly towards it. The particular issue at the moment was whether we should be prepared to sell wheat to that nation, given that it was suffering a severe drought and widespread grain crop failures. Of course, the answer seems obvious now. Of course we should, if we could spare the grain and make a profit from the sale.

Back in 1963, though, ideology interfered with this simple logic. Australia and America were Capitalist states, and the Chinese Communists were seen as baddies who were intent on bringing down the free world as we knew it. One of the aims of American foreign policy was to rid the Chinese of their Communist leaders and philosophy, and to replace them with the American way. So, our Communist-hating Prime Minister Menzies kept on earning brownie points with the US, and docilely followed its lead.

Here we were then, with a surplus of wheat for export, and on the one hand confronted with a near-famine in China, but on the other, we were quite reluctant to trade with the evil, Communist Chinese.

At the start of 1963, argument on this was really on the boil. I will illustrate this by quoting from two Letters from the Sydney Morning Herald, (SMH) that put very different points of view.

Letters, D Droulers. Australian Wheat Board member Mr T Shanahan says he cannot understand objections to the wheat sales to Red China. I have no doubt that he does understand full well, because anyone with any knowledge of the realities of the world cannot fail to see **the dangerous political implication** of this sort of trade.

It is only a few millions to begin with and then it grows, as trade can very often grow, to such proportions that no democratic

Government would be willing to risk the sudden economic shock that the curtailment of these sales would bring about.

In such a situation, how could we then resist the political pressures that would inevitably come? These may be slight at first, then, as trade increases, we see less and less reason why we should not compromise further and so the vicious circle has begun.

I put it to all thinking Australians that our leaders, fully conscious of these great dangers, nevertheless are still willing to risk our security – and perhaps our very survival – for the sake of economic gain and nothing else.

Letters, John Bligh, Qld. A lot of pious, uninformed rubbish is being written about sales of wheat to Red China.

As a wheat-grower myself and knowing that the Western bloc nations have an over-production of wheat, I ask D Droulers, who obviously is strongly opposed to sales of grain to Red China: **is it unprincipled to make wheat available to millions of undernourished human beings, whatever creed or colour they may be?**

It is well known that Asia is in urgent need of farinaceous foods – all evidence points to that fact – therefore, would the West have the moral right to deprive Asia of this sustenance?

Logically, let us assume that Canada, Australia and other Western bloc countries have all refused to sell wheat to Red China. Then the only conclusion we could arrive at would be that those masses, needing food to sustain life, would suffer from further undernourishment and famine. Would the West want that?

I suggest to the opponents of trade with Red China that they drop mere theory, and relate their thinking more positively to the needs of the underprivileged and to the need for wheat farmers to market their produce. Wheat, after all, is the mainstay of agriculture. To suggest that other crops be planted over wide areas instead shows a complete lack of practical understanding of the situation.

The second matter for introduction relates to Australia's policy towards nuclear arms. **On a world-wide basis**, there was the nuclear deterrent argument that said that no other country would dare to bomb you if you had bombs ready to hit back with. **On a local Australian basis**, there were plenty of people who said that we should persist in our attempts to get access to nuclear weapons, while there were just as many who said that if we got them we would become a **magnet** for attack.

There were plenty of different opinions, and suggestions. Some of them were sensible.

Letters, Ralph Summy Jnr. Professor Titterton has indicated that Australia and some of the other non-nuclear nations are at a fateful crossroad. Should they develop an independent nuclear force, or should they integrate their strength into either of the two Super Power blocs?

A third course (not developed by Professor Titterton) is also open and was proposed by the ALP last fall – i.e., the establishment of a **nuclear-free zone** in the southern hemisphere under stringent inspection and controls. Although this is only a localised kind of disarmament, Professor Titterton in his concluding remarks – "the only way (for the great Powers) to avoid proliferation of nuclear weapons would be to negotiate a full disarmament agreement…" – infers that disarmament is the sole responsibility of Russia, the USA and Great Britain.

I believe that Australians cannot escape the responsibility of facing up to the problems of disarmament. They must make a deliberate and reasoned choice. Before embarking on a nuclear weapons program – whether independent or integrated – they must at least ask themselves: **Is a localised disarmament agreement politically and technically feasible**, and would such an agreement be in the best interests of the people of Australia?

Since the nuclear road is a road of no return, I consider these to be vitally important questions.

Letters, Peter King, Canberra. Nuclear weapons will only compensate for a nation's inferiority in conventional weapons if rival nations remain non-nuclear.

The SMH's Editorial "Australia's Problem Of Nuclear Defence" does not discuss **Indonesia's likely response to an Australian program for producing plutonium in uneconomic nuclear power reactors**, but it should be plain to all.

Once Australia and Indonesia enter a nuclear weapons race, Australia's lag in conventional weapons will be as important (or as unimportant) as it is now, but our danger will be vastly greater. It would be as cheap, and far less dangerous at this stage, to spend Professor Titterton's 450 million Pounds on improved and larger conventional forces – if it is really our duty to run an arms race with Indonesia.

Nuclear forbearance will be in our interest during the years immediately ahead. We should use these years to attempt a "localised" arms control agreement, as Ralph Summy suggests.

However, the ALP's nuclear-free southern hemisphere proposal, which he endorses, is neither localised nor "practically and technically feasible." What is needed is an effort to get agreement among South-East Asian countries from (say) Malaya to New Zealand to prevent the production and stationing of nuclear weapons on national soil. (A nuclear-free ocean cannot be effectively policed; a nuclear-free territory can be until the first nuclear weapon is produced on it.)

Such a proposal would mean that Malaya and Australia, in particular, would have to review the nuclear aspect of their alliance arrangements. Britain would no longer be able to base nuclear armed V-bombers in Singapore, and America would be denied port facilities for Polaris submarines in Australia. These features of an agreement would have some appeal for Indonesia and would probably be acceptable to the United Kingdom and the United States.

America, Britain and Russia (because of her interest in Indonesian defence) should be included in the negotiations and could be parties to the subsequent treaty. To involve more Powers than those mentioned would be too ambitious at this stage.

Letters, G Davey. The sub-editorial "Australia And Problem Of Nuclear Defence", following the articles by Professor Titterton, deserves the most detailed study by every thinking Australian.

Whatever understandings we have with other countries, Australia's voice will carry weight in foreign affairs only when she has the capacity to fight with her own defence forces and is equipped – including tactical nuclear weapons – by her own industries as far as possible.

Australia should build a large nuclear power station to provide power for metallurgical purposes and to produce plutonium for tactical nuclear weapons. We can do it and we can afford it.

Comment. Prime Minister Bob Menzies had been fighting, for over a decade, to get into the "Nuclear Club". The initial members were the US, Britain and Canada, and Menzies had hoped that, because we had large deposits of the minerals needed for nuclear explosions, he could blackmail his way in. On top of that, he made large areas of Australia available for British nuclear testing. But, so far, all to no avail, and Oz entry to the Club was not being allowed.

At this time, in 1963, however, Menzies was losing a little of his enthusiasm for this. He could see that other nations were making bombs, with or without the consent of the Club or the UN, and that the deterrent effect was not as great as had been thought. In any case, while he did persist after a manner, his efforts came to nought, and even now, fifty-odd years later, we are still on the outer.

The third matter concerned the great Oz pastime of the idyllic January. England's cricket Test team was in Australia, and were doing quite well. So much so that the future owner of the Ashes would be decided by the Fifth Test. The nation was breathless with excitement, and watched every minute of the games on television on any one of three Channels.

Unfortunately, though, only two hours of play were shown every day, and these same two hours were shown by all three Channels. At the same time, the ABC cut back on its music programmes at times to make way for cricket, so that there was less music, and it was scattered all over the day.

Given this cruel and unnatural deprivation, but not accepting it, there were some spoil-sports who wanted to cut back on cricket, both on radio and on TV.

Letters, Robert Southern. Games of cricket played by men may be as important as games of marbles played by children; but they are certainly not more important. I therefore deplore not only the interruption of musical programs to announce the latest scores, but the amount of 2BL broadcasting time which the ABC devotes to the tedious description of these interminable games. As a music-lover, I would much prefer real music.

I also resent the mixing of games results and so forth into the brief-enough sessions purporting to give "news." Just as the river heights, rainfall records and the Stock Exchange reports are given separately for those who want them, all sport should be separated from "news."

It may be that my feelings are only those of a small minority, but can that be proved? By what objective evidence, if any, can the ABC know the numbers of those who prefer and listen to its sporting descriptions on 2BL, as against the numbers of those who prefer to switch their radios off at such times?

Letters, (Mrs) Margaret Hughes. I wonder if other mothers of school-age children are as fed up as I am with the way Sydney television channels have pushed children's programs off the air, or cut them down considerably in order to show Test cricket. It is not uncommon lately for all three channels to show cricket until 6 o'clock. This is particularly hard on pre-schoolers who look forward to the 15 minutes of the day when they can see something suitable for their age group.

I am particularly disgusted with Channel 2, whose programs I usually admire. They do not have financial pressures to consider, and I think they should leave the field to the commercial stations. After all, we are shareholders in the ABC and surely they must know that cricket fans are not a majority. Mothers of school-age children would welcome a more liberal supply of good-quality children's programs, either as entertainment or education.

Letters, M Calder. In reply to E Williams, surely the very fact that cricket is shown on all television stations for two hours a day whilst the Tests are in progress suggests that it must be extremely popular at that time of day to the viewing public.

I would suggest the "large minority" that Mr Williams refers to could be likened unto a needle in a haystack.

Letters, V Jones. I feelingly support Robert Southern, who deplores the encroachments of sporting broadcasts into 2BL time, which would normally be devoted to good music, interesting talks and discussions. When Parliament is in session hardly any time at all is left.

The talks and discussions are irreplaceable, being mostly topical; but to supply the music I have recently acquired a record player and am gradually getting together a library of records. This is a costly and slow way of making good a deficiency which would not exist if the wishes and the rights of the less vocal part of the community were considered.

Letters, G Pike. Considering that Test cricket against England occurs in this country once every four years and that each TV showing is for two hours each playing day of five days or less if there is an early result, I consider that the cricket critics re TV show a very selfish attitude.

I cannot visualise many children being deprived of TV time because, at this time of the year, the swimming pools claim their attention.

Letters, Mother Who Knows. G Pike states that he cannot visualise many children being deprived of television time because of the televising of cricket. May I say that there are a number of children who are being deprived and should be considered.

I refer to the hundreds of children who are long-term patients in hospitals and in private homes. These children derive more pleasure than healthy children from television shows, because their activities and interests are very limited.

My five-year-old son, fortunately, is now recovering from an illness which kept him strapped to a frame for two years. During this time, the television children's shows were the highlights of his day.

I fail to see how the keenest cricket fan can watch cricket on the three channels at the same time – unless, of course, he has three television sets in his living-room.

BOGLE AND CHANDLER

On January 2nd, the newspapers reported that the bodies of two persons had been found early on New Year's Day, on the banks of a small stream that passed through a popular picnic area in Sydney's prestigious Northern Suburbs.

Police subsequently confirmed that the man involved was a Doctor Gilbert Bogle, a scientist working with the CSIRO. The dead woman was a Mrs Margaret Chandler, a house-wife, who formerly worked with the CSIRO. Both had been guests at an all-night party nearby, and had left the party together.

The man was clothed only in a shirt, and shoes and sox, and his blue-grey suit was neatly folded beside his head. The woman's clothing had been "disarranged". They had died after 4 a.m., though the woman died over an hour later than the man. Her body was covered with some beer cartons, and his body was under some form of carpeting. There was no sign of violence at the scene, though clearly both had been sick and vomiting. It was thought that after the man died, the crippled woman had crawled away, and so there was a definite distance between the bodies.

Police suspected that the cause of death was poisoning, though what that poison might be was not obvious. Their spouses had been at their homes after the party, worrying about their partners, and Mrs Bogle had rung the police, anxious for his safety on the roads.

Over the next few days, and in fact for the rest of the month, there was intense speculation about what might have happened. Not a day of January passed without a major article in the early pages of all newspapers. Initially, it was suggested that the poison had been strychnine, and this had been in capsule form. But there were no empty phials, and anyway, self-administered poison meant suicide. This seemed out of the question to all observers.

A week later, with the poison not yet identified despite much testing, there was the possibility that the couple had been given poison just before they left the party, and this initially had a laxative affect and they stopped their car journey, to her house, to relieve themselves. But this left a lot of unanswered questions, such as who covered them up? And who had snuck the poison into their drinks? And it certainly confounded the majority of people who were convinced that the couple had stopped for immoral purposes.

As the days ticked on, samples of soil were taken and analysed, samples of dust from the carpet were given a similar treatment, and university laboratories were called in to examine body parts. The police issued statements to the effect that they were following a definite line of enquiry, and this was taken as a sure sign that they were baffled. Things got murkier when it was revealed that the carpet that covered Bogle came from his car, parked over 100 yards away.

At the end of the month, Police admitted that they "were up against it." They had spent some recent time trying to find other motorists who had been in the park at the time of their death, but with no apparent success. On top of that, they had not been able to determine what poison had been used, and how it had been administered. In fact, on February 1st, they said that the scientists had given up in their search to identify the poison.

So, it seemed that the cause of this event would remain a mystery. Be that as it may, it still remained newsworthy, and we will return to it as the months roll on.

Comment. This was highly controversial news, and the Press loved it, especially the sensational evening and Sunday papers. All the holiday-makers made the most of it, and for holiday weeks remaining, it was the obsessive topic of conversation. Everyone had their own theory. Most of these involved murder, and most of the suspects were still suspected even though they had clearly been somewhere else. It was a great holiday diversion, and many oldies who can remember this 1963 January will still tell you in fine detail of the gruesome crime and its investigation.

OTHER MATTERS

Often, at the end of a Chapter throughout this book, I will put together a few Letters or news reports that give a glimpse of the absurdities of life this year. Sometimes they are related items, sometimes not. Some are happy. Some are deliberately stupid or provocative, and others are solemn and absurd at the same time. In any case, I will give you a sample now.

Letters, Ernest King, Brisbane. With its magnificent record of achievement, one wishes that the CSIRO would undertake an investigation into the common house or eye fly. Surely, there must be some bird that lives on these pests and could be bred or encouraged to breed.

I still have unpleasant memories of a holiday down south that was not improved by the presence of flies everywhere one went, from Sydney, through Canberra and Melbourne, to Adelaide. And the return journey via western NSW, phew! Flies are increasing, with a consequent increase in summer gastro and dysentery.

Letters, John Boswell, Australian Federation of Sun Clubs. The idea that nudists are food and health cranks running around in the wilderness dies hard.

In fact, the majority of Australian nudists, who belong to the Australian Federation of Sun Clubs, are normal, uncomplicated people from all walks of life, whose sole distinguishing trait is that they can, and do on occasion, meet entirely naked and conduct themselves without loss of composure or a sense of social responsibility.

The overt acceptance of the human body, although uncommon, is not attended by any cult rules, nor is it with any particular philosophy. It does, however, pay tremendous dividends in the easing of tension, in the regulation of many conventions to a more accurate place in social perspective, and in the healthy enjoyment for our children.

THOUGHTS

Comment. A popular family car, the Hillman De Luxe saloon cost 999 Pounds. (Another related car that sold well was the Hillman Minx). On the average wage, it took about one year's wages to buy it for cash, but about two year's wages on hire purchase. Most people used hire purchase.

Letters, Pommie. Having been in Australia a short while I can so heartily agree that the national motto is, "If it moves, shoot it, if it doesn't, chop it down." But we can also add a national emblem.

We were told in England that Australia's national emblem was a broken beer bottle. We laughed then, but we find that never a truer word was spoken. They are everywhere.

FEBRUARY NEWS ITEMS

Let me warn you now. The Queen and her entourage left Britain on the February 1ˢᵗ. She **is coming for a visit to Australia**. That means weeks of pomp and ceremony are in store for us, and while it might charm and thrill many of us, it will be a pain in the neck for others. If you are in the latter group, **there will be no escape here**. You should think about leaving the country.

…---… From Saturday February 2ⁿᵈ, **Morse Code will no longer be used** to send telegraphic messages between our Post Offices. In future, messages will be sent by teleprinters **using alphanumeric keyboards**.

Immigration from Britain has reached record levels. In **January alone**, there were 33,767 applications for assisted passage, and this compared to a monthly average of 9,800 from July to December last year.

Comment. Even if only half of them came, that's a lot of Poms migrating here.

Traffic cops (domes) are being replaced on NSW roads….

The so-called diamond turn will replace them.

In London, doctors at Leeds General Infirmary successfully **transplanted a kidney** from a dead man to a living patient. It is believed to be **the first such operation in the world**. The doctors believe that the operation could lead to the successful transfer of lungs, livers and other organs from those who died.

OFFICIAL WARNING

The Queen is now almost in New Zealand, **and already our local papers are carrying ecstatic headlines.** On February 6th there was the breath-taking news in the *SMH* that "New Zealand prepares a Royal welcome despite showers". This was in the middle of Page One. **Oh, the excitement of it all.**

THE QUEEN'S VISIT

It had been about a decade since the Queen visited Australia. That tour was a raging success, with millions of people taking every opportunity to catch a glimpse of her and her husband, and politicians of all colour vying to be presented to her, or to be invited to the Royal Balls in every State. The common folk lined the streets while she drove past, schoolchildren were lined up in State showgrounds and they waved flags at her, and she obligingly waved back and smiled. A good time was apparently had by all.

It turned out, however, that some people were not really impressed. In NSW, when the Royal Tour for February and March was being discussed, certain killjoys – the NSW Teachers Federation – said that they did not want the extravaganza of thousands of schoolchildren assembling and waving wherever the Queen went. They recalled that, last time round, the children were kept waiting, standing in the one spot for hours, often without water and food, in heat, and all of this for just a glimpse of the Queen if they were lucky. As one teacher's official put it "I do not know who benefitted from this, but it was not the children."

So, throughout early February, they pressed to have the children's assemblies cancelled in NSW. This drew a mixed reaction.

Letters, (Mrs) Dorothea Bremner. In my opinion the opposition of the NSW Teachers' Federation to the children's rally to meet the Queen on March 4 is not only a major insult to the Queen and the Duke of Edinburgh, but also a slur on the loyalty of the thousands of Sydney-siders who are anxious to give our Royal visitors a real Australian welcome.

As the teachers have vetoed this demonstration, and have obviously influenced their pupils to suit their own ends, I would suggest that only those teachers and children who have stated their willingness to take part in the rally be given a holiday on that day. Taxpayers should not be expected to pay wages to those **disloyal** teachers who are only interested in holidays.

Letters, J Phillips. I am thoroughly disgusted with the attitude of the NSW Teachers' Federation towards the children's rally to see her Majesty Queen Elizabeth II and her husband, the Duke of Edinburgh. Never did I think I should live to see the day when teachers would fail to cooperate on such an occasion.

What an insult to the Minister, Mr Wetherell, and the Director-General of Education, Dr Wyndham, to say that the children would suffer by such a rally! They most certainly would not agree to any arrangement that would cause suffering.

With regard to the enthusiasm about the whole thing, that was certainly in the hands of the teachers. Having had over 40 years' experience as a teacher, I know full well you can make your pupils enthusiastic or otherwise about anything. How many times I have had a parent say to me, "It isn't what **we** say, it is what **you** say that matters." I am sure thousands of teachers have had the same thing said to them.

The very fact that the Teachers' Federation circularised the schools soon after they reopened, advising teachers to boycott the rally, put a dampener on the arrangement. What a dreadful thing to do!

Letters, (Mrs) Jean Page. The time has surely come for an ordinary parent to take a stand regarding the rally for the Queen which was proposed by the Education Department and the tour organisers.

First, the NSW Teachers' Federation appears to be the bogy in this case. **Why this body should be condemned** when teachers, of all people concerned, have the best working knowledge of mass movements of schoolchildren, is incomprehensible.

The experience of Mr M Gray, State director of the Royal visit, is probably limited to his own children. The Federation, in the light of former experiences, drew the attention of all concerned to the distressing conditions which would prevail, when the proposed rally was first mentioned. This was the time to be guided by experts who should never have been ignored.

Secondly, speaking as a mother with years of P and C experience and many days spent helping harassed teachers and children to proceed to functions at public grounds (not, however, on public holidays), I can state with certainty that **toilet and drinking facilities are never adequate** and that long queues cause great mental and physical suffering to adolescent girls. Surely Mr Gray doesn't make comparison between 200 children in a group with several teachers in charge and a few parents shepherding their own children to the same amenities on Sydney Show days.

The supposed "insult" to the Queen is laughable. Surely the opportunity is ripe to take this fine, motherly woman – who has expressed her desire to see children – to the Children's Hospital, the Far West Hospital and the Spastic Centre, where the little confined ones could see their Queen. At the same time, we who are able and have fit and well kiddies can perform our own duty and line the route as family units to welcome the first lady.

Letters, Meredith Oakes. I was surprised to read two letters condemning the opposition of the NSW Teachers' Federation to a schoolchildren's rally to meet the Queen. These letters suggested that the teachers were disloyal, that they had influenced the pupils "to suit their own ends," and that they had been wrong in suggesting that the children would suffer by such a rally.

I am a fifth-year High school pupil. I wish to state that, in my school at least, our lack of enthusiasm about the rally was in no way fostered by the staff. The decision as to whether we would attend was entirely in our hands; and having had experience of such gatherings (which, I affirm, are at best chaotic and at worst sheer torture), most of us felt that we could put our holiday to better use.

Our teachers, it is true, made little attempt to awaken our enthusiasm, but I feel that, as teachers, they had no need, in fact no right, to influence us in **a matter so utterly irrelevant to our education.**

As for giving the Queen "a real Australian welcome," it should be obvious that there are better ways of doing this than to assemble children who often are scarcely aware of what the whole thing is about, line them up in the sunshine of early March, and wait for them to faint.

Comment. The mass assemblies in NSW were cancelled. As it turned out, the NSW teachers got a great sense of satisfaction a few weeks later when the Queen was in South Australia. The day of that assembly there was hot, and 75,000 were gathered at Victoria Park racecourse. The children suffered quite a bit, and 250 of them collapsed and had to be treated by ambulance-men. The newspapers were full of shots of distressed children being carried to cooler climes in the arms of their rescuers. I suspect that many teachers, after the criticism they had received for cancelling assemblies in NSW, were quietly very smug about all this.

Letters, P Wood. Now that about 250 schoolchildren, by fainting at a rally for the Queen in Adelaide, have proved the folly of mid-summer mass gatherings, will our "loyal" citizens admit they were wrong after all? I doubt it! They will protest that such suffering – though unfortunate – is outweighed by the renewal of our bonds of friendship with the mother country.

How strong a bond can it be that must be bolstered by this sort of futile torture? What will most of the young victims have to say later about misplaced patriotic fervour?

Those zealots who supported the NSW rally are of a class that wishes – at the expense of others – to demonstrate that Australians can be as subservient to "form" as the English themselves. I believe that the sooner this small-minded type fades away, the better.

Other grizzles over the visit. Lots of people wanted many parts of the queen's itinerary changed for all sorts of reasons. The cost of the decorations, and the cost of the Balls, and the loss of manpower and the cost of the holidays, all came under consideration. Many wanted a change in the itinerary so their own little bit of heaven would get a fleeting visit. This gentleman below had his own beef.

Letters, A. The efforts by those responsible for arranging the Royal tour to lessen the fatigue of the Queen and the Duke of Edinburgh on their forthcoming visit to Australia are highly commendable, involving in particular the maximum use of the Royal yacht Britannia.

However, it is most regrettable that the organisers have not seen fit to provide for the Royal couple to travel by train at any stage of the tour. Instead, all inland travel will be by air. This means that on each journey the Queen will face a public farewell, followed by a short respite of, say, an hour in the air, to land and face a round of handshakes and speeches in a public welcome. While the comfort of air travel is undeniable, this use in this way will be undoubtedly very tiring.

The various railway systems are all able to provide trains with appointments equal to those often used by Royalty in Great Britain. The occasional use of a Royal train would provide a break of a few hours for the Royals, permitting them to see some of the country from ground level.

Moreover, while passing through stations en route, the Queen has merely to stand on the train's observation platform, an operation requiring no mental effort whatsoever, to satisfy thousands of country residents all along the route. These people, who have been shabbily treated in the tour program, can instead have the pleasure of watching the Royal aircraft pass over at perhaps 10,000 feet.

On the occasion of the 1954 tour, the Queen is believed to have stated that she preferred a proportion of rail travel, as it was more relaxing. It is a pity the organisers have omitted this way to make the tour less arduous, as well as more satisfactory to the country people who are to be denied a sight of the Royal couple.

The tour goes on. The Queen and Prince Phillip arrived in Canberra on February 19th, and spent a few days, then off to South Australia for almost a week. Then to Victoria for another week. They were kept busy shaking hands, going to race meetings, cricket, and hospitals, driving past big crowds, and going to a dozens of small cities and towns. They met with crowds of well-wishers, (500,000 in Melbourne), all with small flags, and by men in morning suits and appropriate hats, and arrays of women, **none of whom refused to curtsy.** Up to the end of February, nothing really special appeared to happen, and we can wait breathlessly for some right royal stuff-up next month.

INITIATION CEREMONIES

When young men left home in 1963 to go to live with other young men, in institutions like University Colleges or the armed services, they did so with some trepidation. They knew, that apart from the delights of joining up with other like-minded free-spirits, they had to go through **a process of initiation.** This meant that the older inhabitants, the ones who knew all the ropes, would gang up on them and make them do unpleasant things and suffer serious indignities. This was process that might last for a few hours, or in some cases, for a full year. Sometimes it was just fun, and at other times it was actually cruel and sadistic. But the new recruits were forced to endure it, and rebellion was not commonly contemplated. Acceptance was the price to be paid for entry to the group. Of course, as the years rolled on, the tormented grew into tormentors, and the system perpetuated itself.

The correspondence below shows that it does indeed **take all types to make a world.**

Letters, Parent. The news that Dr Grahame Edgar is going to investigate the initiation ceremony that is meted out to first-year students at Hawkesbury Agricultural College is welcome.

The boy from Perth was unlucky – some students were left alone from 1 a.m. to 4 a.m. to sleep but they all had to sit by senior students at mealtime and as these gentlemen poured salt, pepper and sauce over their meals, students frequently did not get the equivalent of one meal a day. Their hair was cropped to the scalp by these "kings" (as they call themselves) and, during last week's heatwave, no new student was allowed to wear a hat while working in the sun.

Having to crack an egg with an advanced embryo chicken in it on their heads and go straight in to a meal, to drink a revolting and nauseating concoction called "royal cocktail," to kneel on the gravel when seniors arrive for each meal, have chaff dust put down their clothes after they have run long distances, being abused in foul and obscene language at all times by the "kings" – these were, my son said, minor things compared with those which were "too revoltingly filthy" for him to tell us.

If Dr Edgar is sincere in his investigations, I suggest that he interview first-year students away from the college, and that he take steps to protect them from the reprisals which they would undoubtedly receive for telling the truth. Having been warned of reprisals that are long and determined, I will reluctantly sign myself as "Parent."

Letters, John Ritchie. As a graduate of an agricultural college, I am indeed surprised at the amount of publicity being given to initiation ceremonies which have been the general thing at boarding-schools and colleges for many years.

The aim of initiations – to bring all new students to one level so that they can work together as a body rather than congregate in small groups – seems to have been overlooked by journalists and some parents.

As regards bullying, all students get equal treatment and are quite at liberty to object and withdraw from any part of the initiations.

Letters, Dorothy Ramsay. As a parent of one of the "kings" in this year's initiation ceremonies at Hawkesbury Agricultural College, I would like to comment on "parent's" letter. I hope in the two years at her disposal that that parent will be able to do more than I have been able to stop her boy dishing out this treatment instead of being at the receiving end.

Beside me are photos of the initiation of two years ago. They show boys doing press-ups to the point of exhaustion; new boys dragging the seniors in the college coach with the brakes on; boys grouped naked in the sheep dip; boys down on their knees bowed low before the seniors; a senior with a small cigar in his mouth squirting water at a junior with a drenching gun; hair being shaved off into a dish; a group of boys, one sucking a dummy, another with a freshly killed sheep's head on a string round his neck (he is holding it out so it will not spoil his sports coat, which he is wearing inside out); a large group with pillow-cases over their heads preparatory to being led out at night and left to find their way back; boys chewing live frogs.

Everyone I speak to apparently thinks this is a desirable state of affairs. "What are you crying about?" they say. "They have not killed anyone yet. It toughens them up. It is good for the boys." My husband, who is a graduate, defends these practices hotly: "The Minister will meet a lot of opposition if he tries to do away with the initiation practices," he says. "The tradition of the college depends on it."

Well, perhaps there is good in it. I do not know, but I do not think that boys should be at the mercy of whatever devilment the particular batch of students behind them cares to dream up. And if it is all that good, what is wrong with introducing something of the kind into all High schools?

Perhaps it would be all right if there were some standard practice which is acceptable to trained youth leaders, and students went to the college prepared to face a test of their "stick-at-itiveness."

One of the things which particularly enraged me two years ago was that the boys were seized on their arrival at the college and kept incommunicado for a fortnight. Their parents had no means of knowing that they had arrived; nor were the boys allowed to go to the railway to collect their luggage, but had to battle it out in the pig pens in whatever they were wearing on arrival. The new sports coat which graced our son could not be cleaned and had to be replaced.

"Parent," I throw you the torch!

Letters, J Kemp. As a graduate of Wagga Agricultural College, I support wholeheartedly the remarks of John Ritchie regarding the purpose of initiation ceremonies at agricultural colleges.

With an annual intake of 40 or more new students, coming from all strata of society, and with educational backgrounds ranging from the Intermediate Certificate to the Leaving Certificate with honours, there is no more effective way to weld them into a unit, thinking and working as a "year" rather than as individuals, than for them to go through an initiation together.

It should be remembered, too, that those "bullies" doing the initiating have all been through it themselves, and those poor lads, whom mothers are now springing to defend, will not be above initiating someone else when they have the opportunity. Surely no one could object to stunts such as measuring the main street of Wagga with a Frankfurt, or selling bags of manure as a "new organic plant food," and thereby raising 44 Pounds for the local hospital.

I am sure the hundreds of old boys of the agricultural colleges would be the last to want abolition of initiation ceremonies, and that those making the most noise are seeking sensational Press copy, or defending boys who are unlikely to finish the course anyway.

OTHER MATTERS

Letters, R Thompson. I like Sydney, and generally speaking I like Australians, but I have no love for the anonymous Public servant who drew up the forms I had to fill in (twice) to enter your beautiful country as a tourist.

While recognising that to an Australian there is a difference between those holding British passports and those who do not, why don't your officials use a less objectionable description? The word "alien" has offensive overtones; the very next question asks my alias! Could I not just be a visitor with a non-British passport or a foreign tourist, anything in fact rather than an "alien"?

Further evidence that in the official mind the conception still exists that all foreigners are potential criminals is found in your Customs form which asks whether I happen to have with me any coshes, knuckle-dusters, or spring-bladed knives!

Your Australian National Travel association is doing an excellent job selling Australia in USA, where, I confess, it is virtually an unknown country. They told me that the number of tourists to Australia is increasing rapidly each year and that by 1963 it is expected that direct expenditure by tourists will reach 36 million Pounds – of which over 3,000,000 Pounds would go into the coffers of the Federal Government (which designed the forms in question) in taxes of one form or another.

If this Government of yours wants foreign tourists, then why not be more friendly to them? The steward on the aircraft asked me if I was travelling on a British passport. He didn't say, "Are you an alien?" Surely, your government officials could be equally polite so that I, being an alien, could become instead just a foreign visitor. I would certainly like you a lot more if you were a little less insulting.

OZ POLITICS AND THE FACELESS MEN

The Labor Party was a funny animal in the days of 1963. As indeed, it has remained ever since. It was then faction-ridden, with the Left, Right, DLP, and other groups of people all pushing their own policies, often to the detriment of the Party.

One curious mechanism was **the manner of deciding Party policy.** Put simplistically, each State had a group of about half a dozen Party officials, often dubiously elected, who met regularly enough in a national body, and they decided what Labor Party policy would be for the time ahead.

This seems innocuous enough at first sight, but under examination, it has its weaknesses, and these were highlighted in 1963. In February of that year, this National Executive, of 36 men, met in Canberra to decide on policies for the next Federal elections. This was the normal process, but the upsetting part was that photos were taken, and published, of the Labor leader, Arthur Calwell, and his Deputy, Gough Whitlam, loitering outside the meeting, under a streetlamp in Canberra, in the early morning, waiting to hear the results of the meeting.

The press then hammered the Labor Party. What is going on, they asked, when policy is decided by these **un-elected Party hacks**, while the elected representatives of the people are left waiting in the cold? Is this democracy? What's the point of having elections if policy can come only from these **"36 faceless men",** who were almost completely unknown to the electors.

This phrase "36 faceless men" was hammered and hammered over the next few years, and indeed the perceptive ear can still hear it being used to batter Labor.

THOUGHTS

Drinking laws varied from State to State, but they were pretty tough in NSW and Victoria particularly. In NSW, at present, all pubs had to close by 10pm, and were closed on Sundays. But that State had a **curious provision** that they must all **close between 6.30 and 7.30pm, for a so-called meal break**. Now, the **Government was removing that break.**

Australia has dropped from third **to fourth in beer drinking statistics.** The Brewers Society said that Belgium was number one, then West Germany, and New Zealand. Britain was fifth. The measure used was **consumption per head of population**.

A so-called dance craze, **the stomp,** was sweeping the nation.

This involved standing in the one spot and stomping your feet in time with some very loud music. **Heaven forbid that any dancer should touch any other**. Nearby residents called the police and wrote Letters. It was a professional renovator's dream.

Buckingham Palace today confirmed that **Prince Charles** had **a cherry brandy at a Scottish hotel. The 14-year-old heir** to the Throne ordered **a brandy** before a meal at a place called Stornoway. He was there with his schoolmates from the *Gordonstoun* training ship....

The serving of alcohol **to persons under 18** was illegal in Britain. The Palace would not comment on what disciplinary action, if any, would be taken against the Prince at the school.

MARCH NEW ITEMS

Professor Marcus Oliphant, gazing into the future, said that Australia should **use nuclear power to de-salinate sea water** and hence revive our arid lands. Lots of people were quick to point out that the venture would be immensely costly, and that **it might be better to build more dams.** In any case, **you** will be aware that **neither idea has been acted upon since.**

It was revealed today (in headlines) that both the US and the USSR were **making spy flights on the other nation's ships**. **Comment:** What a surprise.

The NSW government is legislating to **allow aborigines to buy liquor throughout the State.** Previously, they could only do so if they had applied for a certificate of exemption to buy alcohol. Currently, **only 1,500 aborigines hold such certificates**. The Chief Secretary, Mr Kelly, said that "it has taken 20 years for the Government to make this grudging handout of human rights." He also said that it would greatly reduce sly-grog sales.

An article in the SMH pointed out that there was a big change under way in **providing non-police security in Sydney**. Armed and licenced men were now patrolling their beats by van at night and **were replacing the patrolmen and watchmen who were resident on the work-site.** The Miscellaneous Workers Union objected to the rapid growth in this type of security. The main providers were SNP (Sydney Night Patrol) and Metropolitan Security Services (MSS) who are still prominent is providing security services.

Comment. This has been a great growth industry. Just look round any shopping centre and count the number of guards who are visible, and guess how many others there are involved behind the scenes.

Tanya Verstack, probably Australia's most popular Miss Australia ever, **was married on March 13ᵗʰ.**

Tempers were getting frayed to the north of us. **Indonesia and Malaya were reacting to a proposal by Britain to combine** some of their territories in the region into **a new State called Malaysia.** These States were Malaya, Singapore, Sarawak, Brunei, and North Borneo. While these five nations were variously keen on the idea, Indonesia was opposed to it. Australia had given words of support for the scheme, but was keen to avoid the sword rattling that was developing.

The Queen's tour of Oz carried on in a predictable manner. Whizzing round between States, lots of parades, millions of disappointed patriots who could only catch a fleeting glimpse of her hat, politicians' wives who were ready to kill to get a seat at banquets, 104 degrees in Alice Springs, "dazed and delighted" in Perth, back to Sydney to sail away tired but happy in the Yacht Brittania on March 28ᵗʰ ....

Of course the Tour was rated by all those who had a hand in it as "the best Royal Tour ever". It must have been exhausting for the Queen and Duke, but they fronted on all occasions, with **good grace and undoubted charm....**

Somewhere during the five weeks she was on our shores, the Queen found time to **bestow a knighthood on** our favoured son, **Robert Gordon Menzies, our Prime Minster.**

HOOLIGANS AND OTHER TEENAGERS

On March 17th, Sydney's newspapers reported that a party at Lindfield had been crashed by 500 teenagers, who proceeded to "wreck the joint". Apart from the normal grog and vomiting and punch-ups and groping, there was the added delight that the cops were called, and that they had some difficulty gaining control over the damaged scene. All over Oz, similar events were reported weekly, as well as bashings on trains, abusive and threatening behaviour at night, and hit-and-run raids on shops. The youth of the nation, it was said in many quarters, was out of control.

It was obvious that the **numbers of teenagers** coming towards adulthood was increasing as a result of the Baby Boom. But that alone should not be sufficient cause. Speculation was rife about what other factors were involved. The most common cause was generally found to be parental laxity. This was **sometimes** seen to be deliberate, with some parents determined never to deny their children anything. **At other times**, it was seen to be the result of moral weaknesses of the parents, who were described as simply not paying enough attention to their children or not caring enough. Such parents were also accused of setting bad examples themselves. Lack of discipline had its supporters as well.

On the other hand, parents had their defenders.

Letters, Parent of Teenagers. Once again parents are being condemned by some authorities as mainly responsible for juvenile delinquency.

It is quite disheartening for parents who are trying to cope with rebellious youth to receive nothing but blame from the Judiciary and the Churches, especially when parental authority has been so whittled away by the law.

Parents are urged to discipline their teenage children, yet the law allows children of 16 years to leave home if they can support themselves, and at 18 years parents cannot even prevent their children leaving home in any circumstances. Under these restrictions how can parents confidently exert strong discipline?

As a sop to parental authority, it is necessary to secure their permission to marry under 21 years, but this permission is so often secured under duress because magistrates are only too willing to override parental objections, or the daughters may threaten to leave home anyway.

Few parents are physically capable of giving their teenage children the kind of punishment they so often deserve, and if they do mete out such punishment, they risk losing their children altogether, or perhaps even being charged with assault.

If parents were more effectively supported by the law, they could more confidently impose the necessary discipline.

The two writers below saw the causes of delinquencies in the entertainment now watched so avidly on TV.

Letters, A Knapp.   What are the driving influences in this trend towards brutality? Might not one of the main factors be our various forms of entertainment, where savagery, corruption and death are shown on an ever-increasing scale? So-called "amusement" that extols brawn instead of brains, thuggery at the expense of law and order, and vice instead of virtue, cannot fail to have a deleterious effect on impressionable youth if absorbed in sufficient quantity. Young people are largely products of their environment and will come to accept violence as a normal part of life if it is presented to them long and forcibly enough.

Is it not probable that youths, continually seeing the main characters on the screen and in comic books ready to knock a man down or shoot him at the slightest provocation, subconsciously form the idea that this sort of action makes them "men," earns them admiration and attention, and qualifies them to live in an age where **might is continually portrayed as right?**

Letters, R M Fuller. How far do the television industry and the publishers of lurid crime novels contribute to juvenile lawlessness? Consider the many TV shows that devote themselves to gangster stories. It may be countered that this is not a new matter, that child delinquency has been a problem of all generations, so its prevalence need not be laid to the alleged decadence of moral and social ideals of the present day.

But it cannot be denied that never before have television stations and publishers so intensely exploited crime. TV trailers again and again use the words "romance," "adventure" and "thrill" in plugging a new crime series. Is it a cause for wonder that impressionable youngsters may at times dramatise themselves in the deeds of enemies of the public good?

True, most television and possibly a majority of the fiction tales show the wrongdoer as being punished, but it may be asked whether it is not high time that television stations and fiction publishers realise their social responsibility, to say nothing of their moral duty, to stop casting a single ray of glamour over the deeds of underworld characters and of evil-doers, young and old, who are increasingly terrorising the community.

This is not to say that it is wrong or even unwise to write screen stories that are based on crime. The Bible contains such stories and the best of writers have often produced them. But it is one thing to portray a criminal in his true light, and quite another to set him slyly on a pedestal as an adventurer, a bold, brave fellow, and a romantic figure.

There was no shortage of proffered solutions. Some of them were sensible, some not. I suggest you try to work out which is which.

Letters, P MacCabe. During my teens, boys from 14 to 18 years of age compulsorily served in a cadet corps for drill-periods of four hours approximately every third Saturday afternoon, and for two hours one evening each week throughout the year. On their eighteenth birthday, youths transferred to the compulsory citizen force until 24 years of age.

As cadets, we learned the basic principles of parade-ground drill, how to handle a service rifle, how to shoot and how to behave ourselves. Many of us grumbled and many of us, like myself, later served as volunteers with the First AIF abroad.

In recent years, in densely populated areas both in the country and cities (particularly in Sydney and Melbourne), hooliganism and larrikinism have become dangerously rife in streets, milk-bars, parks and on beaches, and have given parents and police alike growing cause for alarm. Lately, in Sydney especially, this menace of louts on the loose has developed into something approaching gang warfare reminiscent of the organised "pushes" of Surry Hills and the Rocks areas of earlier days.

Would not the reintroduction of an Australia-wide system of compulsory military training (say, for all physically fit youths from 16 years of age) reduce hooliganism to a minimum and also provide healthy exercise and instruction to our young manhood?

Letters, Repatriated Australian. First, may I state the obvious by saying how tragic it is that these poor, immature rockers must be taken seriously – youngsters so lacking in moral fibre that they must band together like frightened chickens for Dutch courage?

However, since their nuisance value simply cannot be ignored, I believe that **the weekend gaol sentence**, as practiced overseas, should be introduced to cope with these types of offences. I saw the terrific impact made by the introduction of this penalty, certainly the most dreaded sentence of all.

The prisoner is forced to continue his normal working life, thus avoiding hardship to his family, but each Friday he reports direct from his place of work to gaol and stays there until he is released on Monday morning in time to begin work. Also he serves every public holiday in gaol.

To my knowledge, no one has been sentenced to longer than two years' weekend imprisonment, and even that was considered too harsh as the strain becomes so great. However, I do feel this sentence could have a very chastening effect on rockers and similar youthful types.

Letters, Vincent Fairfax, Chief Commissioner, Boy Scouts Association, New South Wales Branch, Sydney.

I can speak as one with intimate knowledge. Membership of the Boy Scouts Association in New South Wales amounts to 42,000, which is nearly 10 per cent of all boys between the ages of 8 and 17. Quite properly not every boy wants to join this voluntary uniformed movement, but waiting lists and a geographical study suggest that at least 15 per cent would be Scouts if they got the chance.

The association is well organised to train leaders and establish new units. We are making great strides and could do much more if those on the sidelines, who appear so "concerned about youth," would do something about it. Like any other growing movement we need the personal services of men and women together with financial contributions and, or, organised backing from firms, clubs, institutions, Churches, and other bodies.

A great number of the stated problems could be resolved, and far fewer children would need "drastic attention", if there was stronger public support and recognition of the existing youth organisations whose programs contain a degree of decent moral influences.

Letters, A Healy. The article "Challenge to Youth" on the voluntary services, given by youth of the advanced nations to the backward parts of the world, rightly drew attention to the lack of any comparably organised scheme in this country.

Elsewhere, private and semi-official schemes of a similar kind have operated for many years, and official sponsors have had a basis on which to build.

In Britain, for example, it has long been common for young men and women to spend a year between school and university in socially useful work. I have come across numbers of them doing elementary school-teaching in the African colonies. This experience is in itself a contribution to their own education.

Something of this kind badly needs to be sponsored in New Guinea. If fares were paid, accommodation of a simple kind provided, and a nominal salary equivalent to pocket-money guaranteed by the Government, hundreds of volunteers would surely come forward.

This would assist the Territory immeasurably, not only directly through their activities, but also in bringing enthusiastic youngsters not imbued with "old settler" attitudes into touch with the native peoples.

Comment. Have things improved since then? Sometimes I hear the news and think they have become worse. Yet, I look round, and realise that I am surrounded by wonderful young people everywhere. Of course they are as silly as a bit of string, and do crazy and foolhardy things. But I know they will grow out of that by the time they are fifty or so. So, on balance I am an optimist and believe that, **overall**, our young folk are getting gradually better. **What do you think?**

GOODIES AND BADDIES

America and Russia were still caught up in the Cold War. I hardly need tell you that this meant that they were trying to prove that Capitalism on the one hand, and Communism on the other, was the way to go. So they were lying, deceiving, conniving, bullying, threatening, and posturing towards each other and the world, and behaving like arrogant teen-age boys who had not had the benefit of a good belting or two.

At this time, they were both talking about the best way to stop the other party from bombing the hell out of them. Long-range missiles were coming into play, and it was becoming imperative that these could be detected as soon as they were launched. There were also Polaris-type submarines plying the world's oceans, and it was considered a good idea to keep track of these, friend or foe. The Americans were setting up communication bases all round the world, and we, as their ally, were now considering whether we should have such a base on our shores. The proposed site was on the North-West Cape of Australia, well away from inhabitants, and it was proposed that it should not have any nuclear capacity itself, but that the equipment there would be very sophisticated so that it could well become **an immediate target for destruction if hostilities started.** Even if there was no material damage to this nation, the prospect of a nuclear cloud loitering for years was decidedly unattractive.

There were all sorts of questions raised by the prospect of a base at the North-West Cape, and Letter-writers responded with a large volume of Letters. I can only present a small sample of them here.

Letters, P Crossley. Is it too much to hope that the ALP will show more appreciation and generosity towards the proposed establishment of a United States naval radio station at North-west Cape than they did in their blundering negotiations in 1948-49, over the Manus Island naval base, when the then Labor Federal government virtually forced the United States to withdraw all naval forces from the South-west Pacific Area by denying them a necessary base?

We now have a chance to make amends, and to boost our defences, by acceding to the new proposal for North-west Cape, and it is to be hoped that the Labor Party, at all levels, will approve the new base, rather than campaign for the votes of those who, misguidedly or otherwise, would seem to aid our potential enemies by denying our true friends room to establish vital facilities in the Australasian area.

An American naval radio base in Australia, coupled with the nuclear submarines under its control, would achieve, at very small cost, an uplift in our defences which we could not match with the expenditure of an addition 200 million Pounds a year over and above our present defence vote. And all we would have to provide is a few acres of our vast continent, 2,500 miles from Sydney or Melbourne!

Letters, E Gale. With regard to the American base in north-west Australia, I am amazed and alarmed to find that the Government can take such a step without consulting parliament and the electorate. We still know nothing of the details, e.g., for how long is the lease and on what terms? Does it mean an abrogation of our sovereignty?

On balance I think having such a base will increase Australia's danger. A more practical approach to our defence would be to join with other nations in the southern hemisphere and agree to make this a nuclear-free zone, as was once so helpfully suggested by Mr Calwell.

Letters, S Kelly. Dr K Fowler questions the wisdom of granting the US the use of a base at Learmonth. His principal complaint is that "the construction of such a station will decisively place this country in the American nuclear camp."

This statement shows a lamentable lack of knowledge of the declared aims of Communism. As far as the Communists are concerned, we are in the American camp now. And most of us find the company of the Western democratic nations very congenial.

Our survival as a free nation depends on the survival of America. Are we then to let her shoulder all the burden? I feel certain that we won't.

Letters, G Branson. The proposed American Communications base at North-west Cape is vital to the defence of not only Australia and the USA, but possibly the whole free world.

Since **it is axiomatic that the USA would never start a nuclear war,** her strategy, oft declared, is based on her ability to absorb the first nuclear bombardment and blast back. This requires maximum dispersal of her control centres.

At present the Hawaiian Islands and San Francisco are the main USA bases in the Pacific, but last year we saw the Russians "shooting up the range" towards Hawaii with ICBM rockets. As a result of these tests, it is a fair assumption that the exact ballistic requirements for hitting the target have been calculated.

A second "Pearl Harbour," this time with nuclear warheads, would reduce the base to contaminated chaos in a few minutes. Such vessels as were at sea would be without a naval base, and the Commander-in-Chief Pacific without communications or headquarters, and all the South Pacific would be in deadly peril. The proposed base in Australia will make an invaluable "second strike" headquarters.

Nothing could conceivably be of greater advantage to us because its defence, and that of Australia, would become an essential part of American strategy.

Letters, Joseph Firth. It is quite obvious today that the only defence is nuclear defence. Do these starry-eyed adolescents really believe that if Australia lies flat on her back with all four paws in the air and screams, "Don't hit me, I'm defenceless," our aggressively inclined neighbours will be impressed?

The **Indonesian dictator** will decide by expedience alone whether to invest in nuclear arms or not. He is not the slightest bit interested in Australia's attitudes as he knows he has nothing to fear from us. An Australia armed with nuclear rocket-firing Polaris-type submarines would deter any aggressor, but a "nuclear-free" Australia would not be free in any other way for very long.

Letters, Colin Le Tet. The Exmouth Gulf base will have the essential function in wartime of maintaining radio communication with Polaris nuclear submarines. Now each single Polaris submarine carries nuclear missiles with a total destructive power which is greater than the total of all of the explosive power used by both sides in World War II. No one will want to deny that these are fantastically powerful units, and it follows that one of an enemy's first objectives would be to try to destroy them – or at least to destroy any radio base communicating with and controlling them.

So that once such a Polaris-controlling radio base is established on Australian soil, we Australians will have to reckon on being bombed within the first hour of an atomic war breaking out. This makes the statement by the Prime Minister, Sir Robert Menzies, that the function of the base will be to maintain radio communication with naval vessels appear to be the understatement of the century. The Leader of the Opposition, Mr Calwell, has come much closer to the truth in his statement that Australia will face "annihilation without representation."

The Press and Parliament must now make the question of the establishment of this base a primary issue. If Australians are going to be put into the position where they might be killed at any tick of the clock, they are at the very least entitled to have had the opportunity of a democratic vote to decide the issue.

Letters, F Wigelsworth. Correspondents who visualise a nuclear aggressor taking time off to make punitive raids on nuclear "clean" nations lose sight of the most important factor, namely the time element.

There would surely be no choice to an aggressor in a nuclear war but to concentrate on areas where retaliatory sites were located, and the first 24 hours of a nuclear war could determine the future of Australia without a single weapon being directed at us.

Sir Robert Menzies would no doubt consider it impudence for Australia to expect to be consulted as an equal by the United States in matters of American foreign policy, yet we seem to be committed to participate in any war at the drop of a fanatical hat in Washington.

Should we be honest and admit that we are fast becoming a United States satellite, we are proud of it, and damn the consequences?

Comment. The whole issue was tied up with dozens of questions. Should Australia try to enforce a nuclear-free zone? Who were we in danger from – Russia, China, or Indonesia? How well could we defend ourselves without America's help? Should Australia make herself a target this way for a nuclear attack? Did the population know the full facts of the base? These issues, and others, were all muddled up. In the long run, the base was built. At times, over the last 50 years, there have been **protests about it**, and also a more secretive base built later near Alice Springs (at Pine Gap). **But to no avail.** Still, if you go by results, no damage has yet been done, and all of the dire predictions have not been fulfilled. I can live with that.

OTHER MATTERS

Letters, D Macfarlane. I wonder do all "Grannies" feel like I do after minding their grandchildren?

I have two rooms, and invariably after minding them I just flop down anywhere among the devastation and have a cup of tea and forget one of them, the latest babe, has been in my bed. Result, I get a shock when I go to bed to find it not made.

Sometimes a friend calls, and I feel ashamed at the chaos everywhere, but I hardly have the energy to tidy up. When I do go to bed I find tin soldiers, rubber ducks, and teddy bears in with me and then I begin to laugh and dream about the "Teddy Bears' Picnic."

Sometimes I go to bed with them in the afternoon if they are two-ish and before I realise it they have brought a fleet of cars with them and I find my tummy is being used as a switchback.

This is the penalty of the maidless era – and I wonder do all 60-year-ods get as tired as I do? I would like a holiday with no one under 60; is this selfish?

Letters, E J Hansman. I agree with D Macfarlane about tiredness at the end of the day after minding the grandchild or grandchildren, but never grumble when I think that I have given the mother at least a rest or respite for a few hours. I consider the young mothers of today the heroines of our generation, with practically no domestic help apart from labour-saving appliances and grandmothers.

Another point is that how sad and envious we would be if we had no grandchildren to love and take an interest in our old age. In fairness to this other granny, I must admit that two rooms are not adequate for the liveliness and exploring nature of young children, so why not take them to the nearest park or playground?

Letters, Dorothy Seldon. D Macfarlane must make some changes in her baby-sitting because she is most certainly being imposed upon. She sounds a dream of a baby-sitter and no wonder her services are in demand.

However, I suggest that she look after her grandchildren in their own homes – then the chaos and an unmade bed would be someone else's worry. Also, let her be sometimes unavailable. After all, she will be more appreciated if a paid sitter has to be engaged occasionally.

No doubt she is forging an enduring bond with her grandchildren in this close contact she has with them and for that many grandparents relegated to the fringe will envy her.

Letters, John Leggat. Recently I travelled by train from Nowra to Sydney and was favourably impressed with the comfort of the carriage and the speed of the journey.

The same could not be said of the catering service on the train, for while the young waitresses were courteous and attentive, there was one stupid regulation that said a traveler, even though he had lunched at Nowra, could not buy a bottle of beer, without the accompanying biscuits and cheese.

The young lady said that she had, quite often, been abused by unthinking passengers for a stupid regulation which she was only doing her duty by enforcing.

When will the various Government department officials wake up and stop pushing the poor public around?

Letters, J Horner, Hon. Sec., Australian-Aboriginal Fellowship, Sydney. Congratulations on the editorial "Aborigines' Quest for Full citizenship".

The new bill amending the NSW Aborigines' Protection Act will, when passed, make the legislation fairly up to date. A major thorny difficulty in the way of assimilation and equal status is the provision in our Act, common to all the State Acts, that **no white person is allowed on any aboriginal reserve for any reason whatsoever. This will not be amended.**

While it is agreed that some control of entry is essential, if potential perpetrators of fraud and confidence tricks are to be kept away, yet discretion is necessary. Not all visitors to aboriginal reserves are villains. There are now 17 "assimilation associations" in the country town of NSW. Every member of these voluntary bodies is by assumption a friend of the aborigines, but whenever a member enters a reserve, to visit a friend, he is committing a criminal act.

This contradicts the Government's assimilation ideas, surely. It is time that conditions were made easier for reserve people and their white friends to meet.

APRIL NEWS ITEMS

The Treasurer, Harold Holt, announced that Australia would **move to decimal currency in February, 1966.** The basic **unit was as yet un-named,** and there was no decision yet on whether it would convert from one unit to the Pound or at the rate of, say, two to the Pound. Also undecided was **the name of the sub-unit** (currently a penny), and how many sub-units would be in a unit. Currently, there were 240 pence to a Pound.

Several States, **including NSW and Tasmania**, have been given permission by the Department of Customs and Excise to start **growing opium poppies for the production of opium**. These will be for trial purposes, and will be in small quantities. They might in future be used to create morphine for medical purposes.

On April 11th, **Winston Churchill was made an honourable citizen of the US.** The fact that he was "honourable" meant that he could not vote in elections there. **Nor become President.**

April 12th. A US Navy nuclear submarine, *Thresher*, with 129 men on board, was feared lost on a routine dive 250 miles off Cape Cod in Massachusetts. It was apparently lost in water that is one and a half miles deep. There was little current hope that rescues would be possible.

Betting in NSW and most other States was legal **only at the racetrack.** There you could bet with a bookmaker or on the Totalisator….

Using the tote, **a Sydney barmaid** on Saturday placed a five Shilling bet on the double of Persian Puzzle and Cold Cuts.

When both won, **she was the only punter to have coupled the horses,** and she collected the tote pool of 24,824 units. That is, a prize of about six thousand Pounds, or about 400 weeks of wages. **A good day at the races indeed.**

April 13th. The Navy confirmed that **all 129 of the men aboard *Thresher* were dead.** It said it may never know the cause of the loss.

A 17-year-old boy, who had been receiving blood transfusions for six months, left Wadley Blood Center at Dallas Texas. He **had received 933 pints of blood.** Doctors believed this to be a world record.

The situation in French Indo-China was always precarious. **Vietnam, Cambodia, and Laos, and also Thailand,** were under threat of armed rebellion from forces aligned to **nationalism and Communism.** Many people there wanted to be free from colonial rule. It would currently surprise no-one **if conflicts in the region worsened.**

Hornsby Council (in Sydney) asked the Commissioner for Railways to provide **women-only carriages on trains**. "Overcrowding on trains has made travel uncomfortable and unpleasant for many women, many of whom said **they had to stand because of overcrowding.**" The Commissioner said he would consider the proposal, but he never did do anything....

Comment. Times change, and in the year 2019, half the population (male and female, without favour) have to stand most of the way during peak-hour.

THE MEDICAL PROFESSION

Doctors were in the spotlight this month.

The changing role of the family doctor. Up till about now, all country folk and most city folk had an easy relationship with a family doctor. Typically, when you needed treatment, you went to his surgery, which was in his home. A red light over the gate signalled that he was in. His wife greeted you, and asked about members of your family, and after waiting an hour and a half, you got to see the doctor himself. He greeted you with your Christian name, and asked about your family, and then got down to business. Generally, **he listened to you**, and suggested treatment. Often you walked out with some drug or other that he had got from a salesman, and rarely with a referral to a specialist or other service. Then, if you needed a home visit, he would come round in the afternoon, and even was available for middle-of-the-night visits.

Things were, **then**, in the early stages of change. These overworked doctors saw the advantages, for tax and recreation reasons, of forming into partnerships of two or three. This reduced the likelihood of getting your own doctor in an unplanned visit. And this meant that the doctor became less familiar with your family, and indeed, less interested in it. At the same time, they were becoming somewhat resistant to home visits, and especially night visits. As medical technology of all sorts abounded, referrals to specialists and services increased, and the local family doctors tended to lose track of what was happening to their patients. The one thing that remained steady was the long wait in the surgery, even though by now the making of appointments was becoming more common.

A Senator Ormonde describes his experience:

Letters, J Ormonde (Senator), Sydney. Thirty years ago I worked in the mining industry. For an outlay of 2/- a week, paid into a Miners' Hospital fund, two stays in hospital cost me nothing other than my contribution to the fund. I had my appendix removed for this weekly contribution – today the hospital charge alone listed for the removal of my appendix is 21 Pounds. There were never any worries about medical bills on the coalfields. I played tennis with my medico without embarrassment. My appearance in his surgery and his visits to my home were also met out of a 2/- contribution to a mine-workers' medical fund.

Coalfields medicos seemed more than happy about the set-up. One beloved and highly skilled doctor always turned on a nine-gallon keg of beer for the fund's committee at the quarterly meeting when he called to collect his cheque. The beer was not a bribe either. After a strike, the first payment on return to work was back money to the doctors and the hospitals. The death rate was not any higher in that social set-up in the coalfields than it was in Sydney and the prestige of the medical profession was really high.

He went on criticise the various attempts, by the Government, to work out **these crazy new medical insurance schemes** that, for a premium, covered your costs for medical and hospital treatments.

Letters, J Ormonde (Senator), Sydney. I wonder if modern organisation has not cost the medical profession something in prestige. Group organisation of doctors for taxation purposes and purposes of justified leisure has been a mixed blessing for our doctors.

Doctors are possibly as highly motivated as ever, but impersonality, which comes with organisation, has hurt the medical profession. There are still plenty of good and just doctors of course. But if we have light and shade among medical men there is no light and shade in the modern organisation surrounding medical and hospital benefits. It is all against the public.

Judging from the complaints I get from constituents, medical benefit funds are nothing else than a debt-collecting agency for the medical profession, with the public only getting half insurance when they originally contracted into these funds to get at least 90 per cent insurance.

Doctors in emergencies. The NSW Government was trying to pass legislation that would make it a punishable offence for doctors to refuse to respond to emergency calls. It was saying that if a doctor did refuse, he would have to establish that there was a good reason for doing so, or else his licence to practise would be withdrawn. That is, **he would have to prove that he was in no position to turn out.** Given the fact that witnesses would be few and maybe biased, this seemed quite a difficult task.

Over and above that, there were objections. Doctors and others complained that most middle-of-the night-calls were frivolous, and were hardly necessary. They complained that they would then be required to attend to patients 24 hours every day, for 168 hours per week. They said that this was nationalisation by the back door.

Others reflected on the perceived breakdown of the doctor-patient relationship.

Letters, G Nagy. The proposed legislation to compel a medical practitioner to attend to an undefined emergency under legal threat will do more harm than good. The conscientious doctor has done his best in the past and will do so in the future, irrespective of circumstances; the exceptional unscrupulous one will find means to pass responsibilities to his more willing colleagues.

This legislation cannot seriously affect doctors as they are facing their duties in traditional manner. Admittedly, in the future, a practitioner may find himself in the degrading situation of being compelled to prove his innocence and professional integrity whenever a crank or malicious person lays a charge against him, but I am far more concerned by the infinite harm this legislation will cause to the doctor-patient relationship.

The practice of medicine cannot be compared with the work of a highly trained technician. The basis of good medicine is still the doctors' understanding and compassion and the patients' trust and confidence. In the past, a doctor was guided by his sense of responsibility, knowledge and judgment to fulfil demands for his attention. This voluntary service gave him a sense of satisfaction and contributed to the all important patient-doctor relationship.

In the future, the medical practitioner will be compelled by law to attend any call if labelled "emergency." "Emergency" being undefined and indefinable, unscrupulous members of the community will make doctors attend when no genuine emergency exists. The patient-doctor relationship will undoubtedly suffer when the mutual trust and respect will be replaced by compulsion and recurrent unreasonable demands.

The real sufferers will be the people who will be deprived of all the intangible benefits gained from their more close relationship with their doctors. Heaven help us if the practice of medicine will become only a technical perfection and soulless.

Let us hope that it is not too late to formulate legislation which will help improve medical care, instead of a short-sighted policy which will undermine its fundamental aim.

The diminishing political influence of doctors.

A number of people pointed out that the considerable political influence of doctors would be reduced as treatments became more impersonal. At the moment, it was easy for doctors, with their prestige and easy and familiar relationships with patients, to influence them. In future, if the current changes persisted, this might not be the case.

Liberace again. As you would expect, there was the money-is-everything comment.

> **Letters, C Le Poer Trench.** My heart bleeds for these poor doctors! After playing to a full house, Liberace, when he received criticism, "cried all the way to the bank." I suggest doctors "cut the cackle" and do the same.

Comment. The Government in NSW was forced into **dropping** the "onus of proof on doctors" clause from its legislation. This meant that, in effect, nothing was achieved by its passage. It was just as well. It seems to me that part of the legislation was inspired by purely cynical political considerations. It was designed to capture the votes of many malcontents at the expense of fewer doctors. I am sure that the vast bulk of the population were pleased when the clause failed to pass.

Since 1963, the doctor-patient relationship has deteriorated markedly, and I don't need to spell that out. The one area that it is most obvious to me is when I visit a GP, and start to relate my problem, it only takes a minute before that doctor starts to scribble out a referral to someone else. I do not know really if this is a good way to go, but the old-fashioned relationship that I grew up on has often weakened.

DECIMAL CURRENCY

The Government's decision to go over to decimal currency had been mooted for a long time. The main reason given was that multiplication and division by 100 simply involved the movement of a decimal point by a few places, and so the arithmetic was simpler. At the moment, the arithmetic involved numbers like 240, 12, and 20, and so was so much harder. Then on top of that, there were those who argued that our new major trading partner, the US, had a decimal currency, and that moving towards a similar currency would streamline trade.

The Government had not, at the moment, decided to use the decimal system for weights and measures. Here, the argument for conversion was in fact much stronger than in currency. Divisors and multipliers were awkward numbers like 1,760, 22, 16, 14, and 454, and lots of others. The arithmetic certainly would be much simpler. But this conversion would need to wait for even longer than that for the currency. Note, that the US, though, had the old imperial system for weights and measures, so that if we were arguing that we should go decimal because of uniformity with the US, the argument fell down here.

In any case, a period of three years was to be allowed for everyone to get educated in time for decimal currency, and for accounting practices to adjust, and new money to be coined and money to be converted. In this period, there was obviously a need for much thinking, and the first issue, in the public mind, was what the new unit of money should be called.

There were plenty of suggestions in Letters. For the main unit, austral, anzac, clipper, whaler, decal, crown, pound, merino, phillip, brolga, snowy, jumbuck, digger and others were proposed.

There were plenty of other writers with ideas equally as valuable.

Letters, R Morgan, Headmaster, Pittwater House Preparatory School, Manly. I hope the Government will soon tell us the names of the proposed decimal currency units. With only three years before its introduction we are already planning our new schemes of money arithmetic which we shall have to implement at once and this is difficult without knowing the names of units.

I hope, too, that the authorities will not be influenced by any of the ridiculous names suggested so far, the adoption of any of which would add another item to the list of aspects of our culture and way of life which already provide basis for international laughter.

Surely there is no good reason why the major unit cannot still be called the "pound" and the term "cent" seems the logical one for the hundredth part of the pound.

Letters, S Wauchop. While in agreement with R Morgan that an early announcement of the names of the new decimal currency units is of vital importance to planning for a smooth changeover, and that many of the suggested names would "provide a basis for international laughter," I cannot agree that the major unit should still be called a "pound."

This would require, in all international transactions, the prefix "A" to differentiate it from sterling and other "pound" units. Similar objections apply to the use of the term "dollar."

What is needed is a name which has both Australian and international implications and connotations; a word which is short, euphonic, easily pronounced and easily symbolised; a word which would be internationally respected.

Such a word, I suggest, is to be found by contracting the word "Australia" to "Astra." This word both retains the sequence of five of the principal letters in the name of our country and is an ancient and honoured word in its own right; it has poetic and patriotic significance for Australians in whose flag stars play such an important role and typifies the spirit of a young country "aspiring to the stars."

This lady below had a much better idea, I think.

Letters (Mrs) F Thomason. By the time we have adopted the decimal currency, HRH, the Prince of Wales will probably have come to full responsibility, so why not adopt **Welsh names** for our coins?

A penny is ceiniog, which in course of time could become familiarly known as a noggin. A shilling is un swllt, which might be known as a schooner. Ten shillings is deg swllt. One pound is penadur, not so very different from the English.

For the benefit of those who favour a "two-headed penny" we could have dau pen ceiniog (dau being pronounced more like die) and all sorts of variations could ensue from this. Five pounds is pum punt. 100 Pounds is cant punt.

At least these names would be the actual names of coins, not animals!

Apart from this lively discussion, other Letters argued various points of view. I present a collection of these below, though I must say in some of the early ones I found the thinking woolly and a bit scattered. Still, their preferences were clear enough.

Letters, Max Mansell. I note with regret and some apprehension that the treasurer, Mr Holt, proposes to introduce a decimal currency into our Commonwealth, not by the obvious, simple and least costly method of basing it upon the current monetary system, but by introducing a new unit based on a 10/- unit.

It must be obvious to everyone, except the Commonwealth Government, that by basing the currency on the present Pound the only replacement of coins which would be necessary would be the doing away with the penny and halfpenny (which are worthless anyway), and also our present useless threepenny piece.

The replacement of these coins by a cent (or groat) equivalent to one hundredth of a Pound (i.e. 2.4d) would enable us to change over to decimal currency, retaining all existing paper money and silver coins, which could be replaced from time to time by new titles; it would enable all existing calculating machines to be easily converted with a minimum of trouble or expense; it would enable all existing balance-sheets and monetary statements of all accounts to be retained in their present form, necessitating only conversion to the shillings and pence (i.e. the least important part of these things) into their decimal equivalents.

If this conversion scheme is **too simple and obvious** for our Treasury Department to understand I would be very happy to explain it to them. Please leave our pound alone – it has been devalued quite enough already!

Letters, H Dudley. Why should the Federal Government change over our currency without even consulting the people, and without a referendum?

The cost of 50 million Pounds could be better laid out on the defence of our country; what would be the use of such currency should we be taken over by another country close at our back door?

Letters, J Donovan. Ever since I found out that we will definitely change to decimal currency, I have been having a quiet laugh to myself wondering how the businessmen are going to work out the guinea which has been a great little money-spinner for all concerned.

Letters, Bob Boase. Which is the easier to work out: the cost of two articles at 1/2 each or the cost of two articles at 0.24 auster? Which is the easier to work out: 8½ yards at 9/11½ or 8½ yards at 2.39 auster?

We are just about to spend 30 million Pounds finding out that there isn't any real difference.

Letters, (Mrs) M Holmes. Please let us keep our present nomenclature for the new decimal currency, changing the values appropriately, otherwise a savage blow will be struck at the very heart of our culture.

What, I ask you, will become of "Pounds, shillings, and pence, the monkey jumped the fence"? And how are we to "Take care of the pence and the pounds will take care of themselves"?

"In for a wombat, in for a roo" hasn't the same alliterative power as "In for a penny, in for a pound," and I can't say I like the idea of "One a bunyip, two a bunyip, hot cross buns," though I notice that these traditional Good Friday confections have already been transformed into Easter buns anyway.

Then, what about sport, so important in the Australian way of life? Shall our little girls sing "Mother, mother, give me an austral," as they skip? And what, oh what, is to happen to the swy game without double-headed pennies?

Comment. Some readers might remember that at the turn of **this** century, there was a great hullaballoo about all our clocks, and trains, and trams, and lifts, and banking, failing because our timing devices would not handle the new digits in the new year. Well, in 1963, the introduction of the new currency had something of the same proportions. But, despite many a warning that disaster was upon us, the conversion in 1966 went very smoothly and it seems, all the automatic vending machines, and indeed the entire economy, coped very well, thank you.

OTHER MATTERS

Publicans and aborigines. In NSW, it was now legal for aborigines to be served in pubs. But that does not mean that they were suddenly welcomed with open arms.

Letters, Dymphna Cusack. It was stated in Parliament this week that a publican from Kempsey said "Whether we like it or not, the aborigines are **not** going to be allowed to just walk into a pub and get a middy. I don't know of one hotel in certain North Coast towns, including Kempsey, where they are **not** going to be served."

In other words, the law of the land is to be flouted. Do the hotelkeepers pick and choose which laws they observe?

By all means, expel the badly-behaved people, whether pink, puce, corned-beef coloured or aboriginal, from our hotels, and thereby raise the standard which visitors from England, Europe, Asia and Africa expect. But let us not place ourselves in the distressing position of President Kennedy who was forced to send US marshals to enforce the law made by his own legislators for the black students in Alabama.

Letters, S Sekel. On Tuesday, my wife entertained about 20 women at a fund-raising luncheon. Imagine my disappointment when, on coming home, I found the kitchen lino pitted with stiletto heel holes up to half an inch deep. I now fully understand the precautions taken by the management of the new Fisher Library at Sydney University, where no heels smaller than a shilling are allowed.

If more places applied this rule, it might force shoe manufacturers to produce sensible shoes again, and women to wear them.

THOUGHTS

It is apparent that **Pope John II is becoming seriously ill.** Vatican bulletins are being issued daily, and they say sometimes that he is in a critical condition, and sometimes that he is feeling much better. The prospects are not promising.

When it came to naming the **new currency**, a Letter-writer from Waverley pointed out that Australians have the habit running adjacent words together. Hence "an egg" becomes "anegg". Likewise, we get anorange, anapple, and so on. If our major unit of currency became **an austral**, what would that sound like, he asks? **Decidedly on the nose.**

WHAT VIEWERS WERE WATCHING: Thursday Night

	CHANNEL 7	ABC	CHANNEL 9
6.00	Superman	True Adventure	Ripcord
6.30	News	Spy King	News
7.00	My 3 Sons	News	Comedy Play
7.30	Jacky Gleeson	Maigret	Stoney Burke
8.30	Hitchcock	Lorrae Desmond	The Nurses
9.30	Laramie	UNI of the Air	Dave Allen
End	Reflection	Spy Catcher	Religion

Comment. A five minute religious talk, usually with a prayer, closed off every day's off viewing. If you did not want to see movies, there was not much viewing on a Sunday night.

MAY NEWS ITEMS

The former **Dutch territory of West New Guinea** had been administered by the United Nations over the last seven months. On May 2nd, **control of it was transferred to Indonesia**. It is now named West Irian....

The *SMH* editorialised that for the first time in history, Australia now **had a land boundary with an Asian nation**. That was in New Guinea....

The *SMH* editorial also **showed our paranoia about the Communist so-called menace.** It said that if Indonesia turned Communist, we would be at great risk from threats from that quarter. There was no doubt that the Reds were making serious efforts to gain some control over Indonesia, but the Herald was much more alarming than the situation justified....

In any event, **50 years have passed**, and there has been **no military invasion across our borders.**

May 8th. Donald Campbell's attempt on the land speed record would have to **hurry up**. Floodwaters from Queensland were slowly spreading towards Lake Eyre, and there was still **plenty of preparation work to do.** In a few days, Campbell would do his first trial run at 75 mph, and see how it all goes.

A New England New State Movement was established to agitate for **a new State to be carved out of NSW**. The area affected would be in the north-west of the existing State, in the New England area. The Movement built up considerable support, but in the long run, came to nothing.

Since WWII, similar new States have been proposed right round the nation, but **our maps remain un-altered**.

May 10th. The *Bluestreak* reached a speed of **210 mph. May 12th, it reached 250 mph**. The nation was on the edge of its seat, while the floodwaters moved steadily towards the Lake. Only a few more days were available, the racing team thought.

On Sunday, May 19th, the Sun Herald had **the headlines "MORE RAIN EXPECTED."** This was in large block letters, and was followed up with associated stories of local flooding and sports events cancelled. For example, on Page 5 the headlines there were that jockeys at Randwick race meeting had been blinded by a spray of mud. **WOW!**

Then there was a story that America's latest **astronaut to circle the earth had taken a pep-pill before beginning the descent.** You might gather that this was a quiet news-weekend.

May 21st. Donald Campbell was forced **to cancel his record attempt for a year**, because of the flooding of Lake Eyre. The Bluebird would be stored at a near-by station for that year.

The Sydney City Coroner, after **the inquest of Bogle and Chandler,** decided that they died from **unnatural deaths, with acute respiratory failure.** "But as to the circumstances under which such failure was brought about, the evidence adduced does not enable me to say."

May 30th. The Sydney Water Board decided **that Sydney's water would not be fluoridated**. This was **against the advice** of just about everyone who could talk.

MIGRATION IS NOT EASY

Mr Robinson, the Commonwealth Migration Officer, pointed out that we had taken in 75,000 persons from the United Kingdom in 1961, and 95,000 persons in 1962.

Comment. That is a lot of people for a small country to absorb. Obviously, the number had grown over the last few years and, on top of that, for the first quarter of 1963 it was running at the rate of 134,000 per year. This meant that there were hordes of families living in hostels for long periods, and many of them could not get suitable jobs. There was a great deal of disappointment, and this was often borne with stoicism, and sometimes with a lot of whinging. A growing number were packing up and going back to likely misery in the UK.

One aspect of this was captured as below.

Letters, Dorothy Bremner. Much is written about helping migrants, but a small paragraph in Rev D Wilcox's letter says so much: **"More interest needs to be taken by private people."**

I have the opportunity of speaking to women, members of the Mothers' Union throughout the dioceses of Sydney, about migrants. I have discovered that it is not that people do not care, it is that they are not aware of the conditions and life of migrants living in hostels. How many of our people realise what it is like living a community life or what it is like when your child cries in the night and his room is a separate one down the corridor, and to take him to the "toilet block" is probably to walk 200 yards in the rain?

After the initial shock, many of the migrants adapt themselves to hostel life because most have made this great step in their life for the sake of their children's future, but, working among the mothers, I have found that what they need and appreciate most is friendship. They are not wanting charity, but friendship from one woman to another, to be invited into a home, to drink a cup of tea out of a pretty cup (after thick white china), to walk from room to room, to have someone to talk to and answer all the questions they are longing to ask about their new country. I have found women who have been in Sydney 12 months and more who have never been inside a private home. Statistics show that if the migrant mother is happy and content, the family stays content. I have seen how women at Bradfield have been helped by the friendship of churchwomen at West Lindfield and Killara, and I have found that once you interest people and show how they can be of help, they do this readily.

Somehow we must make our whole community realise that many migrants can be helped to settle into our community and be happy, by all of us living up to our reputation of being "hospitable people."

Letters, F Robson, Commonwealth Migration Officer, Sydney. Dorothy Bremner highlights a very real need in the migrant's first weeks, or even months, in a new land. As she said, many migrants can be helped to settle in Australia by the hospitality of Australians, and the country's "Good Neighbour" movement acts on the recognition of this fact.

Workers with this nationwide movement, the formation of which was sponsored by the Commonwealth Government in 1950, seek to ease the loneliness felt by migrants on their arrival. They achieve this through personal contacts, by asking migrants to their homes, and by introducing them to clubs and voluntary organisations.

Some 10,000 men and women work voluntarily in this field through the "Good Neighbour" movement. Its offices in each of the State capitals, and its representatives in more than 300 towns and centres throughout the country, will gladly assist people wishing to become part of this vital work to learn how they may effectively help to make "Australian hospitality" a meaningful term to the migrant. "Good Neighbour" work is not a preserve of specialists. It has a place for all warm-hearted Australians.

Comment.   This was the period when the slogan "populate or perish" held sway. At the same time, migrants were on the way here from Greece and Italy. Most of these settled in cities, and the Greeks headed mainly for Melbourne. These brought with them their own problems. For example, many of them were well educated, but found their qualifications were not accepted in Australia. Many of the older migrants made little effort to learn the language for decades, and spent their days among their own communities, ignoring the Oz community around them.

With all these problems, though, and given the sheer number of people pouring in to the country, the migration program of these days was remarkably successful.

As an aside, I mention that all of what I just said **was about the Poms and the Europeans.** None of it was concerned with Asians for the simple reason that we took in virtually none of these.

ARE YOU BEING SERVED?

The Public Service.   Service in Oz in 1963 was not a well-understood concept, in certain jobs. For example, the Public Service, in its remote offices, was always under criticism for its lack of civility, its slowness to respond, its arbitrary decisions, its obscurity, and its refusal to use any level of commonsense in its pontifications. Also, out in the real world, you could be pretty certain that the person behind the counter in the post office, or the station master in the country, or the person collecting tickets at the gate, would be surly and officious to anyone except friends.

Country pubs. Persons touring the country areas right round the nation were always writing Letters about the standard of our country pubs, in an era before motels had really taken off and provided competition. The fact that most rooms had no toilets or running water, and the remote community bathrooms, galled a lot of writers. The beds were invariably terrible, with more than their fair share of bugs and red-back spiders lurking. The noises from the drinking areas below provided quite a learning experience to a few.

To top it off, there was the attitude of most publicans. These persons, male and female, were mainly interested in selling grog, and providing accommodation and services to travellers was something forced on them by licensing laws. Generally, they each had a handful of waifs who lived permanently in the pub, who every day did their bit to ensure the publican made a decent profit from grog. Letter-writers often objected to sharing bathrooms with these "degenerates", as one woman described them.

But back to the publicans themselves. Here is how one writer saw them.

Letters, K Ewin. My husband and I had a very interesting experience on Tuesday night last; we stayed at a hotel for the first time in five years.

Because the motels were full, we booked into a three-star country hotel. To enable us to return to Sydney the next morning, we asked for an early breakfast. Mine Host smiled nicely, and said he "wouldn't dare ask a chef to prepare an early breakfast these days." Could we be called at 6.30 a.m.? Oh, no – there would be nobody about then.

Our bill, paid in advance, included the breakfast that wouldn't be served – 2 Pounds each to sleep for the night. I need hardly mention that the bathroom in this first-class hotel was at the other end of a different corridor to the one in which our room was situated; that is taken for granted in a hotel.

The unhelpful landlord and the temperamental chef must surely work themselves out of jobs very soon, and the general public can only benefit from such an occurrence.

Comment. I am afraid that Mrs Ewin would have been wrong in her last paragraph. The publican and his cook would have survived for many years, and indeed there are **still** many persons in the trade who have clearly been cast in their image.

Sydney's Taronga Park Zoo. Things were no better with this family at the zoo.

Letters, (Mrs) Y Colyer. Could anyone offer a reason why the catering at Taronga Park Zoo is so archaically operated and so inadequate to public demand?

During the school holidays I took my children to the Zoo for the day. Since our last visit (when we took our lunch) I noticed great development in animal housing and display; **but** when we went to purchase luncheon we found:

The dining area with about two-thirds of its tables operating and a stationary queue of at least 40 people waiting. One refreshment bar only was open to sell **only** soft drinks, ice-cream and sweets to both the outside public and waitresses serving at the dining-room tables. The other refreshment bar closed.

Round the corner we found yet another queue of people waiting to buy meat pies, sausage rolls, sandwiches and tea to take away, and hot water.

We waited in this queue for half an hour to buy our simple lunch. There were four women serving behind a bar, but the small space and inadequate equipment (the hot water was boiled in an ordinary domestic copper) made it impossible for them to cope with the numbers of people. Upon requesting two chilled bottles of lemonade, we were informed: "Oh, there's **nothing** cold!"

Surely Taronga Zoo can be regarded as a public utility as well as a show place visited by a great many local and overseas people each year. In this case, it must be in everyone's interest to modernise its catering system, so that it may match the excellence of the animal display and surely the most beautiful site in Sydney.

Perhaps by allowing a contract out to a progressive catering firm to serve simple foods, the Zoo could be made not only a more pleasant place to visit, but might help the many overseas people who visit it annually to realise that we are **no**t a nation of incapable muddlers, but **can** run our public utilities efficiently.

Comment. An old scholar told me that Australian men had an attitude that carried over from history. He argued that, given our convict ancestry, we had a resentment to all authority, and that this had been exacerbated in the World Wars by serving under British officers. That meant we were unconsciously egalitarian to the extreme, and wanted everyone to be a mate, with no one in a superior position. Thus, he went on, Oz men made the world's worst waiters, because that position required a measure of deferment that they would never accept. Maybe he had a point.

LETS GET TOUGH ON TROUBLE-MAKERS

The wharfies. Strikers continued to have their fun. By this time, the coal miners, long held to be villains in this respect, were well and truly behaving themselves, leaving the wharf labourers to champion the cause. All sorts of bodies and tribunals and advocates had tried to tame them, but to no avail. Their leaders, almost all Communists, had been badgered, taken to court, imprisoned, and castigated by almost everyone, again without results. Their menace continued, and some people, including the Liberal Government, said that they really had an agenda to bring in a Communist state. Obviously the politicians did not believe this, but it made good election fodder at the right time.

So, it was time to take drastic action, said a few. Here is one proposal.

Letters, Ronald McDonald. There is only one way to end the present anarchy on the waterfront, and that is to do what a past New Zealand Government did when it had to face up to similar disruptive tactics on the New Zealand waterfront.

The Government passed a law through Parliament to deregister the NZ wharf-labourers' union. Then it called for volunteers to take their jobs. Since that time there has been hardly any trouble on the NZ waterfront.

In order to avoid, if possible, the dislocation of industry which such legislation would cause, the Government could let the wharf-labourers' union know in advance what it intended to do if they did not cease their disruptive tactics; if they continued, the Government could then act as I have suggested. It would obviously be necessary for the Government to provide adequate police protection for the volunteers, even to the extent of enrolling special police.

These measures are certainly tough measures, but tough measures are the only ones that could succeed when dealing with tough men of the type represented by the Communist-led Waterside Workers' Federation.

Mail sorters. Mail was going missing in increasing numbers and this was being put down to pilfering by mail sorters at major mail centres round the nation. A proposal was put forward that movie cameras be focused on the sorters while they were working so their activities could be monitored. The idea of camera surveillance was quite unheard of at the time, so the resistance throughout society was strong. Here, though, is one person who thought it a good idea.

Letters, Pillar To Post. I find it hard to understand why the Amalgamated Postal Workers' Union should object to the use of movie cameras or any other device to help weed out those members who help themselves to other people's mail. Any law-abiding body of workers would welcome the means of cleansing their ranks of those responsible for thefts, and which bring their fellow-workers into disrepute.

The Federal executive of the union was quoted as saying the use of cameras was contrary to the "human rights" of its members. May I inquire what the Postal Union's views are concerning the human rights of the public who use the mails?

Finger printing. The idea was raised by a distinguished judge that the clear-up rates for crimes would be **improved if every person in the community was finger-printed, and their prints placed on record.** He argued, from there, that crime itself would be reduced because of the greater likelihood of detection.

Most people did not like this idea. The argument was raised against these folk that if you did nothing wrong, you had no fear of having your prints on record. But this argument, as always, never convinced anyone, and the idea was well and truly resisted. Again, though, here is a voice that supported it.

Letters, R Shelston. I refer to Mr David Roberts' excellent article about fingerprinting.

Clearly a lot of people would object to compulsory fingerprinting, but the article shows there is much to be said for it; and this in the opinion of Judges, highly placed police officers, and others more qualified in the subject than most of us.

There seems to be no prospect of it coming about by public demand; but an alternative is indicated by Judge Harvey Prior, in his reference to **voluntary** fingerprinting. This may not be practicable but half a loaf is better than no bread, and it is possible that a voluntary registration system, in time, would breed itself into (or usefully towards) a total system.

I suggest establishment of a fingerprint register in two parts:

Part A, for **voluntary registrants** having no criminal taint;

Part B, consisting of the existing police register.

Transfer from one part to the other would be one-way from A to B, upon conviction of any crime.

Many people, those with a clear conscience, would welcome opportunity to get into Part A. Apart from the personal and social values, what an **aid to character reference** it could be.

Pedestrians.   Over the last two years, pedestrians were being mowed down by motorists at a great rate. So, all States brought in measures to get greater control over these walkers.   Thus they variously said that fines would be imposed, and strictly policed, if people jay-walked, or left the curb before the lights changed, or walked on the wrong side of marked middle-lines to be painted on city footpaths.   Reaction was swift and sure.

Letters, RAF.   The timely police campaign against pedestrians must gladden the hearts of many motorists, who have been plagued by these creatures. Until now pedestrians have been permitted to amble freely down the streets of this city.

However, the present fine of 1 Pound will hardly curb our pedestrians. A more drastic measure is required, and I suggest a system of pedestrian licences. All pedestrians should carry a legible number plate, fastened either to a special pedestrian hat, or directly to the forehead. At night, which is the time when pedestrians are most dangerous, they should be compelled to wear reflector beads or tape.

Letters, Antigone. Rather than on-the-spot fines, perhaps the Superintendent of Traffic would prefer the use of firehoses at every intersection in order to teach the Sydney pedestrians better discipline. A well-directed jet of water would efficiently stop erring pedestrians before they have committed their breach of discipline, and therefore be a far more real deterrent than a fine administered after the offence. Of course, it would not be so financially rewarding.

Letters, (Miss) A Welsh. Surely, if a motorist is compelled to observe traffic lights or pay a fine of at least 10 Pounds, the law should compel the pedestrian to do likewise or take the consequences. Naturally no driver will knock down a pedestrian if he can help it, but he should not be deemed culpable if the traffic lights are in his favour.

In the interests of preventing accidents, is it not more important to train pedestrians to obey the traffic lights than to harry them for walking on the wrong side of the footpath in order to look in the shop windows?

Letters, T Peterson. And what is the pedestrian supposed (by law) to do when the officer on point duty has allowed too many vehicles to go through, and then gives the "go" signal to pedestrians while double-decker buses, massive trucks, cars and taxis are straddled across the marked foot crossing?

The time-hardened Sydney-sider simply plunges in and battles for his rights, but one has time to feel sorry for the astonished visitor who doesn't know what is expected of him.

Letters, B Thomas. Mr W A Walsh follows a less aggressive code than that recognised by most sports-minded communities, where a pedestrian crossing against a "don't walk" signal is clearly "in play" and is not considered "out of bounds" until he has reached the kerb, or until the whistle is blown. This will happen in the event of an infringement such as two or more motorists converging on this pedestrian. This is a dangerous practice.

It would be unsporting, surely, to compel the pedestrian, as suggested by one correspondent, to wear a target.

Letters, W Mitchell. I would suggest that those people who jaywalk on Sydney footpaths, or stand in groups talking, should be put in towaway trucks and taken to the Eastern Suburbs railway tunnel, handed a pick and shovel, and in no time Bondi would have its railway station.

Letters, G G Cornwell. I assume that, having introduced on-the-spot fines for walking on the wrong side of the footpath, the Government will shortly designate slow and fast lanes for pedestrian traffic.

OTHER MATTERS

Letters, SINGING STUDENT. Last Monday, at the recital in the Town Hall, to my horror, I heard knitting needles at work in the row behind. Looking round, I saw not one but two pairs of needles click-clicking together industriously.

I realise that people must get their knitting done but, surely, if they have to bring it along to recitals, could they please do it before the concert and at the interval.

THOUGHTS

NSW Police are following up on a **theory** that the **Bogle-Chandler deaths** were caused by poison from a **shell conefish** that had caused six deaths in Queensland. Detectives are travelling to that fair State to investigate its toxicology.

Russia put the first woman into space when a tractor-driver's daughter, Valentina Tereshkova, was fired into orbit.

An Italian Archbishop, Montini, was chosen as **the new Pope**. He will take the title Pope John Paul II.

WHAT VIEWERS WERE WATCHING: Sunday Night

6.00 News	**Kiddies Show**	**News**
6.30 Comedy Time	**Melting Pot**	**Disneyland**
7.00	**News**	
7.30	**Oliver Twist**	**McHale's Navy**
8.30 Movie	**Dan Farson**	**Movie**
9.30	**Face to Face**	
10.00 Jack Benny	**History**	**Candid Camera**
End Reflections	**Religion**	**Religion**

JUNE NEWS ITEMS

June 5th. Pope John XXIII died this morning. He will be remembered particularly because he convoked a gathering of the top clergy of the Catholic Church, called **Vatican II** which, in sessions over a few years, examined **the dogmas and liturgy of the Church** and proposed many changes. Many of these changes have subsequently been implemented, and many have not. It has however, **created a divide within the Church** where the conservatives, who oppose changes, are in serious conflict with the liberals, who promote them.

Gough Whitlam, the Deputy Leader of the Labor Opposition revealed some figures for Education. We devoted 2.9 per cent of our national budget to education, as opposed to 4.5 per cent in USA. We had **20.3 per cent of our 15-19 year age-group enrolled as students against 66.2 percent in the US.**

On June 6th, the Federal Government announced that the **new currency would feature Royal as the major unit**, and the minor unit will be called a cent. There will be 100 cents to a Royal. One Royal will be equal to 10 shillings, half a pound. One coin to be used will be the Crown, which will equal 50 cents. **The symbol for the Royal will probably be the capital letter R....**

The Leader of the Opposition, Arthur Calwell, said that the decision was extraordinary, and shows signs of antiquated thinking. "This is not the last word because **the Labor Government will not accept this antiquated terminology**"....

The Federal Treasurer, Harold Holt, gave details of **the 988 suggestions that had been received** by Cabinet for the naming of the currency.

John Profumo, Britain's Secretary of State for War, resigned today for the Cabinet and Parliament. He admitted lying to the Prime Minister, Harold McMillan, when he said that he had not had **an affair with a London model, Christina Keeler.** Keeler had now disappeared under **spy-like** circumstances, and there was much talk that **Profumo's pillow talk had been transmitted to the Russians by Keeler.** *The London Times*, **exuding virtue,** hammed it up by saying "There can be no more lamentable documents in **British political history."**

As the month progressed, **the Profumo scandal got worse.** It appeared the Christine Wheeler was probably **a serious call-girl,** who lived since she was 14 with a neurosurgeon called Ward. He had links to many well-known figures in England, and was now charged with managing call-girls....

Wheeler also had excellent links with a Captain Eugene Ivanov, a Russian Attache, and it was widely believed that he had asked her to get, from Profumo, the date of the delivery of nuclear war-heads to West Germany. **Spy talk filled the air.**

The British Prime Minister was under attack in Parliament. There were assertions that Macmillan had knowledge of the matter for some time, and had covered up to deflect political criticism.

CHURCHES AND POLITICS

A *SMH* Article. The *SMH* presented an Article under the above heading that made interesting reading. It pointed out that over the last few months, the Protestant Churches had argued against the legalisation of off-course betting, the continuation of poker machines in clubs, and the introduction of the evening meal-break in pubs. Also, the Catholic Church last year had failed in its attempts to have state aid for schools introduced.

These defeats for the Churches in NSW came thick and fast, as they did in other States. **Yet they were met by indifference from the public.** In fact, more than indifference – active aggression. For example, a Manager of the South Sydney Junior Rugby League Club accused Archbishop Gough, of the Church of England, of having "little or no knowledge of the make-up of Australians", the Anglican Church of being "a big absentee landlord", and the Roman Catholic Church of raising millions of Pounds from housie-housie, raffles and other forms of gambling. Such attacks were echoed by the public.

The Article raises the question of what had happened to transform the Churches from a force, that could make or break Governments, into something which had been discounted time and time again politically as little more than a nuisance element?

It went on to point out that the Churches had lost power as attendances had dropped. But beyond that, it described the changes in the social situation. Today in 1963, it says, there is increased leisure and spending power, fast transport, better education, low-cost literature, a thriving daily Press, and heaps of cinema, gambling facilities, clubs, TV, radio and live theatre. The Churches have lost much of their following to these.

It pointed out that a wide section of the community was **sceptical about their theological claims** and along with this, it was inclined to **mistrust them on secular matters**. The Churches had lost their secular battles now so often that they were being discounted by the public whenever they ventured an opinion on such matters.

Response to the Article

Letter-writers flocked to give their opinions, and they covered many points not raised by the original Article. Many of them were from clergy.

> **Letter, Rev J Broadhead.** I suggest that the so-called **wowserism** of the Protestant Churches is a presentation of **the highest ideals to men and women**. An old Scottish lady once gave me a definition of "wowser" as one who "wants sincere earnest religion".

> **Letters, (Rev) Brian Heawood.** "The politician" and "our rulers" are essentially **"uncommitted"**, and in this of course they reflect the vast bulk of public opinion. The Churches of NSW, are essentially **"committed"**; they are committed to the unpopular view that moral principles have objective value, and that, consequently, "what is morally wrong cannot be politically right." This is their point of view; and it is the point of view of the founder of Christianity.

> **Letters, (Rev) G Trudgen (Ret.** Bishop E K Leslie, of Bathurst, in his reported address to the Anglican synod of his diocese, made the rather unfortunate mistake of attacking members of the Government as non-Christian.

> The basis of the mistake appears to be the rather unrealistic approach which senior, and indeed most,

churchmen seem to have adopted, that politicians should be expected to base their views on certain so-called moral questions on opinions handed down to them from the sundry pulpit apologists. Moreover they are expected to act on such interpretations by **the ancient methods of forcing, by fear of punishment, men and women to be legalistically good.**

Bishop Leslie wants poker machines legislated against, and because they haven't been, he seems to assume that the Government is non-Christian. He assumes this not only on that score alone but also on the matter of the abolishment of the tea break in hotels and on the matter of the expected off-course betting facilities.

Letters, Robert Baker. What Bishop Leslie, the Reverend Alan Walker, and the NSW Council of Churches' star witness, the Reverend Gordon Powell, lose sight of is that **men and women cannot be made saints by legislative sanctions.** This is something the Government understands far more realistically than our church dignitaries do

One might well add that until the Church realises that its traditional role is to teach the individual what is right and what is wrong, and thereafter to use persuasion rather than legalistic sanctions with which to lead people into the acceptance of right rather than wrong, the Churches and not the Governments of the day are at fault.

But before the Churches can hope even to start such a difficult but necessary task, one must face the fact that **much of the Churches' conception of right and wrong is outmoded, unrealistic, and out of tune** with any higher level of thought beyond the purely primitive interpretation of the tremendous truths uttered by the founder of the Christian religion, who himself rarely, if ever, said, "Thou shalt not" and almost always said, "This do," not as a command but in love-filled hope.

Letters, Kenneth Bathurst, Diocese of Bathurst. On the home front I am convinced that we must summon up our resources for a far more active campaign of evangelism. To say that Australia is a Christian country and that every city and township has its churches is to hide our heads in the sand.

Although the State sometimes gives lip-service to Christian principles, and although a number of our members of Parliament are (thank God) good Christian men, our Governments are not and do not profess to be Christian and the sooner we admit this the sooner we shall get on with our mission.

Letters, J Yorke. The major blame must fall on the Anglican Church with its 50 per cent of the total nominal Christian adherents. If systematic statistics were kept, these would indicate the Church has lost ground over the last generation. The Church, to regain social influence, must take cognisance of Australia's vigorous democratic and intelligent society. The antiquated organisation and teaching methods of the Anglican Church are attractive only to the simple and passive elements of society.

The seventeenth-century practice of parish "livings," which clergy can retain for life, must be replaced by limited contracts of service and retiring ages. Instead of being free agents, clergy must expect to be accountable to their bishops and congregations in all matters and subject to regular inspections.

The sermon, the main method of teaching, might have been satisfactory for tenant farmers of a century ago. Must the modern generation sit in silence through **20 minutes of wisdom and nonsense from the pulpit?** The vigorous mind rebels against **the pretension and pomposity of the classical sermon.** If the Church is to regain these people, techniques of the forum, discussion group, question-and-answer method, etc., must replace the traditional sermon.

Letters, S K Barker. I have read with interest the correspondence in the "Herald" on the subject of the decline of the political power of the Churches.

Mr N May criticises the Churches for "lack of crusading vigour and vitality in what they said and did" in the matter of the blatant social evil of poker-machines. What did he expect them to do? Did he expect them to organise a political pressure group to enforce the prohibition of the machines? They couldn't; nor is it likely that any political party would attempt such prohibition.

Gambling is undoubtedly a social and economic evil which should be controlled as such. Mr Renshaw has taken a step in that direction by taxing some of the profits derived from this evil. He could go further by relating the incidence of such taxation to the membership fees charged by the clubs that enjoy the privilege denied to licensed hotels, and by steeply increasing the licence fee on the 2/- machines.

News item. Dr Babbage said the Churches did not seem to be getting through to the people.

Barely 10 per cent of the population, compared with about 60 per cent in America, attended places of worship on Sundays. There was a great deal of real devotion within the church and much sacrificial giving, but it seemed to having little impact on Australia as a whole.

The Church seemed to be catering more for the converted than for those who needed conversion, he said. Most Australians were attractive, Godless pagans, and the image of the Church had little to commend it.

The typical ecclesiastic was stuffy, timid and unimaginative. The Church had lost intellectual distinction and it **moral and spiritual impact on the community was negligible.** "The tragedy is that we are complacent about it," Dr Babbage said.

"I leave Australia with profound regret, but I do not intend to return."

Dr Babbage had been a powerful clergyman for years. He would now become visiting Professor of Christian Apologetics at the Columbia Presbyterian Theological Seminary, Georgia. Here, on departure, he is speaking out more clearly than he ever did before.

THE UNITS OF CURRENCY ARE NAMED

The Australian Cabinet had decided on the names for the new units of currency. It had called for the general public to make suggestions for the names, and the public obliged by sending in 988 submissions. They appeared to do no good at all, because two of the names chosen, "royal" and "crown", were straight from the wish-list of Sir Robert Gordon Menzies. His well-known and fervent attachment to the Queen and Britain obviously persuaded the rest of the Cabinet that expressions of loyalty were called for, so that these names, probably the least popular of all suggested, were nevertheless chosen – in the best Oz democratic tradition.

The Leader of the Opposition, Arthur Calwell, had a genius for never understanding the constituency. On this occasion, however, he immediately spoke out against the choice, and vowed that when Labor got back into power, it would change the names away from royal and crown. This of course was well nigh impossible, because every coin by then would have their names printed on them, and because the currency would already have been accepted round the world as the Oz coinage. To suggest that the currency might change every time the Government changed was a bit too much, even for Calwell.

But this time, at least his sentiment was widely accepted by the public, and for a day he was the champion of the masses.

However, even without Calwell, the general response was overwhelming. The *SMH* had heaps of Letters on the subject. They were almost entirely opposed to the new names. But I found that most of them were a delight to read.

> **Letters, James Kringas.** The announcement of royal as the name of the new currency unit came as a surprise – an unpleasant surprise. One is tempted to ask a "royal what?" A royal blunder? Of all the names that have been suggested this appeals to me the least, barring such names as roo, wallaby and koala, which can hardly be entertained.
>
> Surely to avoid the public outcry which is bound to follow this decision, taken so arbitrarily by Cabinet, a referendum should be held with perhaps six possibilities to allow the selection of names acceptable to the majority of Australians.
>
> **Letters, A Barnidge.** Royals, crowns, florins? How ridiculous! If we must be tied to Britain, why not call the major unit an "Apron String"?
>
> Obviously, the sensible name for the major unit is "Australian dollar," signified by "A". Minor coins should be in 50, 25, 10, 5 and 1 cent denominations.
>
> To us, crown and florin appear to be useless terms. Even now nobody uses the word "florin" in preference to "two shillings" or "two bob."
>
> The whims of one or two people have been imposed on the entire population, and, as a dinkum Aussie, I wish to lodge a strong protest. There is still time to hold a referendum.
>
> **Letters, G D'A Chislett.** Whether royal is a good choice for the name of our currency must be a matter of opinion which, in a quick census, I have found ranges from a

low acceptance, through considerable indifference to significant disapproval. Younger people are more likely to disapprove than older people.

Our adoption of a currency having royals and crowns as the two major units will hardly be seen as a forward step in the republics of Asia, with whom we have to live and trade. Rather will it appear reactionary.

I am not implying the need for a nationalistic name – the pound will do. However, there is one consolation; in future the road to ruin may be known as a "royal progress."

Letters, R Clark. While I welcome the name of our new currency, I cannot agree on the choice of the names crown, florin, shilling and cent for the smaller units.

In keeping with the word "royal," the smaller units should be called noble (5/-), baron (2/-), knight (1/-) and commoner or "mug" for the smallest.

Letters, (Mrs) Morva Sanders. The "Australian flavour" of the name royal for our new currency must be related to the fact that in almost every Australian city and country town there is to be found a Royal Hotel.

Would it not have been a logical sequence to name the remaining unit "club," "commercial," "railway" and "Tattersalls."

Letters, J Lowe. What's in a name? In the case of our currency, a reflection of our national outlook and attitudes. The name royal does not present the Australian as the self-possessed son of a forward-looking nation, but rather as a child waving a flag by the wayside as the Queen passes by.

Our membership of the British Commonwealth is a fine and useful thing, but there are many who display a stronger devotion to its vestigial trappings than to its great traditions of justice and parliamentary government. The views of these people are being put forward as representative of Australian thought.

Letters, A Paul. It is most disturbing to learn that a change in Government will result in a further change of name in our major unit of currency (Arthur Calwell).

Let us be reasonable and compromise. Modify royal slightly by replacing the Y with a B. The result is robal, a phonogram with many advantages. It is 4-5ths of royal to please the Royalists; spelt backwards it will delight Mr Calwell; and pronounced with a real Australian accent it should win us friends in all sorts of strange places. The inclusion of the B is, of course, typically Australian.

Letters, J Beck. One aspect of the naming of our new currency, which has so far been overlooked, is that there is no guarantee that the monarchy will be retained in Britain for ever, which means we will have, for all time, a name which could have no meaning to our citizens of the future, and indeed to the people of other countries.

It is basically wrong to link the name of anything as important as our currency, which is meant to endure, to some set-up which could conceivably change in the future.

Letters, Lindsay Johnstone. How can Mr Calwell be so ignorant as think that "royal" has no meaning for twentieth-century Australia? How can such republican sentiments be expressed by the Leader of her Majesty's loyal Opposition?

Letters, G Dixon. When Mr Menzies promised to lift petrol rationing and Labor stuck tenaciously to "controls," the Liberals got in. When the Liberals now select royal (R for Rupee) and Labor promises to change that for dollar, I predict that Labor will get in on the strength of that alone.

I am against Labor on principle, because I consider any socialist, no matter how high his standard, is only a pacemaker for Communism, but if Labor promises to change the name "royal" they will get my vote this time.

Letters, (Mrs) H W Stumm. Some reactions to royal – the name of the new unit of money – were seen on TV on

Thursday evening and they are worthy of comment. A young girl had the best answer, viz., the name royal was a good idea and it brought us a little closer to England and keeping our allegiance to the Crown.

Others, unfortunately, said almost disgustedly that it was too British. Let us not doubt that the British way of life has stood the test of time for so many years and kept the British Commonwealth to the fore, and side by side with other senior nations of the world. If royal is too British, as suggested by the youth on the TV, why is it that some 45,000 Australians make the trip yearly to see Britain and the British way of life? They do not go to America in such numbers – perhaps they cannot afford the almighty dollar.

Let us be a little different and not copy others all the time. But to say the royal it is "too British" makes one wonder what some of the coming generation thinks, for surely they must have some British blood in their bodies.

Comment. So now you know all about how we got our new currency. It was approved in June 1963, and has been with us ever since. The good old royal and crown have now become so entrenched in our way of thinking and spending, in 2013, that there is nothing more to be said about them. Maybe.

OTHER MATTERS

Letters, F Van der Does De Blje. I am also a migrant and nearly four years here. **We can't understand where people can get the money to go back to their home country.** We never go to the pictures and "pub"; we have no car and also no installments to pay, but we could not even save 10 Pounds, because life in Australia is too dear and work opportunities too bad!

We hate this country and we understand that we have been faked to Australia by your immigration officers in Europe, but we have also no possibility to pay our fares back. So we stay. And if some one of you ask us, "How do you like Australia?" our answer is: "Beautiful! The best country in the world!" What can we do else? What other answer do you "Australians" expect from b--------migrants?

How would a Jew in Hitler's Germany during that regime answer the question, "How do you like Germany?"

You are too proud of yourself to be able to hear the truth!

Letters, R Johanson. I am sick and tired of reading letters from disgruntled people such as De Blje. I am a small businessman and have had occasion to employ men from time to time, and as far as I am concerned I would not employ a migrant again. I have employed migrants in the past, being of the opinion that every man is entitled to a chance, but in my book now a migrant is not worth a bootlace and as far as tradesmen are concerned, I don't believe Europe have any; at least I haven't met one out here yet.

For the record I am an Englishman out here 19 years. Australia has been good to me and I'll back her against any country.

Letters, L V Bartlett. There is probably a good case for an import licence for Fijian bananas, but the disparaging comment by Judy Tudor regarding locally grown bananas scarcely appears to be called for.

She refers to the local product as hard, green, tasteless sticks, but obviously this is not a true description or Australian bananas just wouldn't sell. Locally grown bananas are good tasting and good eating, but at that the Fijian variety may leave them for dead, as the saying goes.

Let us give credit where it is due and concede that the product of local growers is not without merit. At the same time the importation of a quota from Fiji might be a good thing to urge the Australian grower to improve what we have regarded, until now, as a commendable fruit.

THOUGHTS

There was currently an on-going stand-off in the **US State of Alabama,** where the Governor, George Wallace, was doing all he could to **keep the blacks in their under-dog status.** Riots and deaths were every-day occurrences.

Trading with the enemy. Australia will soon enter into an agreement to **sell 41 million bushels of wheat to China** for thirty million Pounds. Our Mr Menzies might preach all the time about the **dangers of the Chinese Reds**, but he still knows **where Australia's real interests lie**....

A **few Letter-writers never-the-less objected to the sale** because "They will not buy the wheat for our interest, but for their own." Since **their interests and ours are at logger-heads,** we are constantly being told, surely we should not sell.

Other writers advise that the sales will be in the interests of both parties. Both sides are winners.

Letters, N F. We travel around NSW regularly and, when-ever possible, stay at the MFA Motels because they are so clean, comfortable and convenient. But why is it that, whereas all are provided with a Bible, only some of them have tea-making facilities? Not, I hasten to add, that I have anything against the Bible – quite the contrary – but, after a long day's travel, I must admit that both my husband and I feel more in need of a cup of tea than of a session's reading, irrespective of the book.

JULY NEWS ITEMS

A Melbourne-based academic, Professor Winks, urged that **Australia should move away from its White Australia Policy** (WAP). "What I would like to see is 50,000 Negroes in Melbourne. **One of America's greatest assets has come from the mingling of the black and white races**"....

The Professor was an American, in Australia for a six-months period, and was on loan from Yale. He went on to say that "clearly we should abolish the word "white" from WAP. All the countries that criticise Australia for its WAP **themselves have migration policies that discriminate somehow**, and there is no reason why Australia should not have one, but **not based on being white**".

The Civil Defence Officer for the City of Sydney said today that, in **the event of a nuclear attack on Sydney**, pregnant women would the first to be **evacuated to the country**. After them, mothers with children under school age, then mothers with children at school, and finally mothers with teenage children. Any left-over capacity would be used for older people. Evacuation would be voluntary.

There was some comment that, given that there was almost no chance of a nuclear attack, the Officer could probably **spend his time on other things**.

July 5th. The *SMH* was all excited that **an Australian girl, Margaret Smith,** would play **the final at Wimbledon** in a few days against American Billie–Jean King....

July, 9th. Margaret Smith won the Wimbledon final. She was the first Australian woman to do so. From here, and later known as Margaret Court, **she went on to win three times**.

The British, Russian and American big-wigs were meeting in Russia to get a full, or partial ban, on nuclear testing. Ho hum. **We've heard it all before.**

The Labor Caucus in NSW approved **the extension of off-course betting to the entire State**. A computer, called a Totaliser, will do the donkey work, and it will mean the **network of 6,000 illegal bookies will probably collapse.**

A Totaliser Agency Board (TAB) will be set up to oversee the creation of local agencies in all parts of the State. It is expected that taxes on betting will now come to the State.

July 20th.   The Soviet Premier, Nikita Khrushchev, outlined **four proposals to end the Cold War.** They were to freeze the present levels of armaments. Resume negotiations to prevent surprise attacks. To exchange military personnel on an ongoing basis. Withdrawal of all foreign troops to their own borders….

Success of these proposals depended on whether various nations **wanted** to end the Cold War. **Some nations depended on producing armaments for their prosperity.** They would need to think hard before they gave this up….

The first leg of the **above proposal** was **shot down by France's de Gaulle** a few days later. The three main powers were happy with themselves because they had almost reached agreement on the disarmament proposal. Then de Gaulle said that **France wanted to develop nuclear arms as she chose**, and would not accept constraints.

NEGROES AS MIGRANTS AND THE WAP

Professor Winks' preference for 50,000 negroes in Melbourne was not well received.   First of all, people were pretty fed up with Yanks telling us what to do, and why we were all wrong.   On top of that, he had only been resident in Oz for a few months, and here he was commenting on a matter that had vexed thinking Australians for decades.

However, it struck everyone that it was not the time to talk about the good that blacks brought to America. Right now, **blacks and whites were rioting in the streets of Alabama and other points in the South,** black gangs were driving through New York streets shooting up the whites, University campuses were under lock-down and riot orders to quell the physical violence. It was plainly a silly time to be telling this nation of ours that the Americans had a better way. Clearly, they did not.

Mr Downer, the Oz Minister for Immigration, was not all that impressed by Winks. He said that Winks' remarks were foolish and shortsighted, and if they were carried out, would lead to social problems and strife. He pointed to the tragedies and complications with the US's 25 million blacks, and he said he was sorry that Winks had trenchantly criticised an important feature of Australian policy. A polite way of saying "mind your own business."

Letters, Edward St John.   The professor could have been more discreet, and may in some respects have been misinformed, but the substance of his remarks merits our serious consideration. It is not only for the sake of "cultural vitality," but for many other reasons also, that Australians should now be taking an earnest look at the policy which for too long has been regarded as a fixed and immutable article of faith in our political thinking.

Our leaders do not seem to realise that **a new climate of opinion is arising throughout Australia**; the article of faith has been taken off the shelf and dusted down, and is now coming under scrutiny. There is more than a trace of hypocrisy and self-righteousness in our attitude to what is happening in, say, South Africa and the United States, if we are not prepared ourselves to accept and work for a true multi-racial society in Australia.

Letters, John Marsden. The "Herald" reports Professor Robin Winks as telling Australia to change its immigration laws, and saying that he would "like to see 50,000 Negroes in Melbourne." This is a pretty fair start for the young man from Yale, USA. Australians will await with impatience his advice on all aspects of national policy when his opinions have matured at the end of his tour of duty in the Antipodes.

Meanwhile, we may request this youthful world authority on racial issues to reconcile his belief that the mixture of races in the United States is an asset "speeding (sic) our cultural and political vitality" with the stark facts of the murder of Medgar Evers in Mississippi, the dogs and fire hoses set on Negroes in Alabama, the ghettoes of the north, and the Black Moslem claim that white Americans are ripe for extermination.

Letters, W Higgs. Visiting American Professor Winks should have "forty winks" and wake up to the fact that he has grossly misrepresented Australia's migration policy. A section of the Afro-Asian bloc at the United Nations will no doubt welcome and quote his tactless statement.

Comment. Most commentators tore strips off Winks for his obvious bad timing and the crassness of his suggestion. But there were a few thoughtful persons whose response indicated that this nation was starting to re-consider its attitude to our White Australia Policy.

Letters, Milton Osborne. As an exercise in illogic, the frequent claim by our politicians that our immigration policy does not involve discrimination is hard to better.

Mr Downer, Minister for Immigration, states that **some 200 Asians** are admitted to Australia as permanent residents each year – this is but **a tiny** proportion of our total intake of immigrants, and the reasons for its size are claimed to be the difficulties for Asians of adjusting to the Australian way of life.

It is hard to see what other name can be given to the policy, if one does not call it discriminatory. Professor Winks was careful to point out that he accepted the right of any Government to determine who should or should not be admitted as immigrants. What he and all those who seek a change in our policy ask for is the abolition of a situation in which it is postulated that one race in inherently more desirable than another.

How much longer will our politicians cherish the myth that a worthwhile society can ignore the contributions of men and women of all nationalities and skin colours?

Letters, E Ellis. I can never find the arguments for restricted intake very convincing, whoever advances them, be they Asians or Australians. We are always prepared to help our Asian neighbours, but does this justify the complete realignment of our racial policy so as to admit a point of a percentage of the vast numbers of Asia? **Does anyone seriously think taking even 10 million Asians will alter the problems of the remaining 1,500 million?** Not even Mr Ali, I think, would hold that friendship must go so far as to let his next-door neighbours come and take over his house on the pretext that theirs is overcrowded.

We would not like to see a partitioned Australia, like Pakistan and India. We would not like to witness the arrogance of white over black in the impending explosion of a South Africa or in the colour pogroms of the United States. We have a unique destiny in that the capacity of our country to hold population can only be gradually increased in a challenge to the elements – from a people that gradually increases in the same measure. To open the floodgates in such a context is to destroy our birthright and to do immigrants, coloured or otherwise, a disservice.

Letters, Clive Kessler. A disconcerting feature of the current controversy over the White Australia policy is the almost universal tendency of Professor Winks' critics to assert that the USA has no reason to be proud of her own racial situation, and that the past errors and wrongs of racial policy in the USA either disqualify the professor from passing any comment on our immigration policy or allow his remarks to be shrugged away as unworthy of serious consideration.

To attach to the professor some share of the responsibility for the racial situation in his own country may not only be unjust; more important, it is no argument against the opinions he expressed. The readiness with which his critics have implied that the current racial situation in the USA is relevant to the present controversy in that it supposedly renders his views less worthy of proper consideration can only be regarded as symptomatic of the guilt and uneasiness, and hence sensitivity to criticism, of those who support the status quo.

Letters, Non-Reformist, Singapore. So that our immigration policy may not be classed as discriminatory, its critics suggest admitting an annual quota of Asians to Australia. Can any of these "critics" propose any type of quota system that would be non-discriminatory? Indeed, if these people are sincere, they should press for the complete removal of restrictions. If Asians are not allowed to migrate to Australia on the same basis as Europeans, then they will always be able to cry "discrimination."

Another popular misconception is that colour is the only difference existing between Asians and Australians. This is not true, although by merely **suggesting** that fundamental differences do exist some will accuse me of racialism.

The Rev Alan Walker would be the first to criticise Catholic mixed-marriage laws. But how would he feel if some of his congregation decided to embrace the Moslem faith so that they could marry a Malay, Indonesian or Pakistani? And what of the midday Moslem prayers? How would the Australian workers feel on a large production line when all Moslems ceased work at 1p.m. to say prayers? Or the noticeable reduction in a Moslem's productivity during the annual fasting month, when no food or water is taken between sunrise and sunset? What would be the employer's reaction? This problem of religion is just one of the many involved in assimilating members of an Asian faith.

Letters, Stan Blake, Singapore. I have lived in Singapore for years. I daily come in contact with people varying from household servants through to university graduates. It has been my experience that a large number of these people know little or nothing of Australia or its immigration policy. Of those that do, very few appear to hold serious resentment.

When I think of the amount of technical and financial aid Australia has given the recipient Colombo Plan countries, the number of Australian soldiers buried in war graves in Singapore, the crowding to capacity of Australian universities to accommodate Asian students and, right now, the making available to the Singapore Government of a specially equipped rainmaking aircraft, complete with crew and technicians, I think Australia has made a very definite effort to create goodwill in this region.

FLUORIDE IN YOUR TEETH

If you are aged about 50, there is a good chance that you have much better teeth than your parents did. That is because, about 1963, the various authorities started to fluoridate the water supplies to towns and cities, and thus delivered a small trace of fluoride on a regular basis into the bodies of children. While almost everyone now recognises that as a good thing, back then the matter was controversial.

The whole idea of doing this came, not from trials on rats and the like, but from observations. In regions that had high natural fluoridation of the drinking water, the people there had better teeth. In Australia, a few local Councils, in country areas in each State, had earlier added the powder to their water, but to get a clear result would take a full generation. Thus, there was little to be learned from them at this time. Skip forward a few scientists, and you come to the stage in 1963 where Sydney was proposing to pep up their water in this way.

The trouble was that when the members of the Water Board met, **they decided against doing this**. Their decision came as a bombshell. Many scientific and medical arguments had been advanced in favour of doing it, and there were few organised groups opposing it. For a while, it was hard to fathom out why the individual members voted against it, but in a few days the nay-sayers in the public came out in the Press, and voiced their doubts. The battle, for and against, was joined. I include a very mixed bag of their opinions below.

Letters, W A Dowe, Director, Australian School of Social Science. People should be free to neglect their health, or even to injure their health, if they so insist. Possibly Mr Sheahan does not propose to take measures to suppress smoking, drinking alcohol, or over-eating.

The existence of a totalitarian Government which insists on the forcible stamping out of evil would be a far worse disaster than even serious tooth decay. There are ways of voluntarily acquiring the benefits of fluoridation, in a free community, but the means to restore human rights when they are violated are very costly and difficult.

Letters, Keith Smith. While many people opposing fluoride, like W Dowe, are theorising, the teeth of thousands of children in this State are going rotten, largely through parental neglect.

During the past 13 years I have met more than 500,000 Australian children in connection with my radio programs. This had made me something of an expert in a very narrow field. Looking back, my main impression of the Australian child is not one of liveliness, wit or physique, but of a deplorable dental state in which schoolteachers and parents had little real interest.

Recently, it was my pleasure to talk with children in Yass who have been subject to fluoridation for nearly seven years. Yass dentists claimed they had the best teeth in New South Wales; it was apparent to me that their teeth looked better than any other group I had seen in Australia.

I am sure Mr Dowe would not condone the thrashing of a child by a brutal parent because it infringed on the parent's "human right." Neither should he confuse the practical protection of children's teeth with the theoretical "rights" of adults, many of whom don't care what happens to children's teeth, anyway.

Letters, Margaret Gale. With the growing number of experts concerned for the welfare of myself and my family, the day seems not far distant when freedom of choice will be blocked entirely. This seems of far graver concern than the preservation of teeth.

Is it or is it not true that in America the incidence of dental decay dropped noticeably after a 12-month trial of fluoridation, but that after five years the "experts" were wondering whether there was some connection between fluoridation and **bone malformation**?

At what point **are the "experts" absolutely sure? Thalidomide is too recent a hurt to give one iota of attention to what the experts think.**

Letters, R Frenkel. Thirdly and finally, the phrase "compulsory medication" seems to have aroused much hypocrisy. When one bears in mind that fluoridated water would taste, smell and look no different from untreated water, and that its effects would be revealed only gradually among those now young enough to benefit, and not at all among those too old, and that in 50 years sound teeth would be taken for granted like the air one breathed, then I confess I see little that is totalitarian in this picture.

Try as I might, I cannot look on unavoidable physical health with any horror whatsoever.

Letters, E Dark.   In a fluoridated water supply there could be no uniform dosage, as the man doing hard work in a hot climate would inevitably absorb a very great deal more of the drug than the sedentary person in a cold climate. That fact would seem to condemn fluoridation as an unscientific way of giving the drug when an accurately calculated dose could be given **in tablet form**.

The protagonists of fluoridation refuse to admit the practicability of this alternative method, claiming without a jot of evidence that mothers would be too careless to give it; but my experience is that the modern mother is most concerned for the welfare of her child, as evidenced by the very high proportion that are immunised. Why should not the same result be obtained with an intelligent campaign to educate parents to give fluoride to children of an age to benefit by it?

Another point that has been ignored is that with the proposed fluoridation of water supplies about 5 per cent of children will suffer from **a brown mottling of the teeth**, for which disfigurement there is no remedy.

The time during which artificial fluoridation has been tried is far too short to justify the dogmatic statement that no eventual ill effects can be caused; in animal experiments with continued minute doses of mildly toxic substances, it has been found that in some cases the ill effects are not apparent until the second generation.

There is also the moral point, which has been far too lightly brushed aside – that no man should be compelled against his will to take a substance which he believes may be harmful if he has to absorb it during his whole lifetime.

Pardon the poor image, but you can see that zero fluoride in water gave good growth, and higher levels produced poor growth.

Comment. You can see that those who rejected fluoridation constantly referred to the idea of freedom of the individual to make his own choices.

The gradual introduction of Fluoride did proceed in a piecemeal manner over the next decade. But it was all so slow, and some hold-out communities maintained their position up to the turn of the Century. Queenslanders, in general still oppose it, even in the year 2013.

OTHER MATTERS

Letters, (Miss) N Jobson. Reading of the translation of the four Gospels into pidgin English for the Papuans, I am reminded of the expression of the Commandments in similar form for the kanakas on Queensland plantations before kanaka labour was abolished. This may interest some of your readers:

Man have God, one fellow; no have 'nother fellow God.

Man love God first time, everything else behind.

Man no swear.

Man keep Sunday very good, day belong big fellow Master.

Man love father and mother belong him.

Man no kill.

Man no want Mary belong 'nother fellow man.

Man no steal.

Man no tell lie.

Suppose man see something good belong 'nother fellow man, he no want him all the time.

This version was taught by one who was the means of the conversion of many boys on her plantation to the Christian religion.

The boys enjoyed their Sunday gathering with its sing-song, little prayers and repetition of the Commandments and simple little talk, and often as they went off said "Goodbye, Missis. Good fellow day. Come again next week."

Letters, P Bartlett.   Just to give one small instance, recently I was trying to reach a friend. Twice I received a tone resembling a musical electric clock. The third time a recorded voice told me to check the number I was calling and get through to service faults should I have difficulty. The fourth attempt I did actually get through to the number I was ringing. I was told that she had lifted her receiver twice but the line had been dead. In this case I presume that I would be charged with two numbers I did not make.

I then endeavoured to get through to service complaints. The first two diallings brought forth complete silence. The third time I received the dialing tone, but on the fourth attempt I did eventually get through, I was told that an engineer would ring me. They will check, etc. Perhaps for a couple of days everything will be right again .... If I am lucky. Needless to say, crossed-lines are an everyday occurrence.

Cannot anything active be done about the situation which I consider a gross disservice on the part of the PMG Department?

Letters, Yoong Soo Pin. Ever since my arrival from Malaya, I have observed with great interest the numerous outbursts regarding the White Australia policy. Thanks to Professor Winks, the "old faithful" made another appearance. Again many put forth the same old arguments either for or against this much-talked-about policy. After five years of stay in this "wide brown land", Australia is as "white" as ever.

The world we live in is a ruthless and selfish one. "Love they neighbour as thyself" and "all men are brothers" seem to have lost their meaning and application. Each nation is pursuing her selfish aims in order to survive in this destructive world. Australia has every right to do the same. She has the right to stick to her immigration policy if she thinks that this will be best for the nation.

If Australia were to be forced to modify her immigration policy and adopt a quota system in admitting coloured migrants, these unfortunate people would not be regarded as equals. **They would be looked on as intruders, parasites, niggers and yellow bastards.** Life for them would be better in their own countries, although they might have to tighten their belts and live in overcrowded surroundings. Unless the Australian people wholeheartedly agree to let in their African and Asian neighbours, it will be better for them and for this country that the White Australia Policy remain as it is, though it may be politically unsound and morally wicked to many in Australia and overseas. When this general opening of the door will come about is anybody's guess, but let us hope that it will be soon before it is too late.

Letters, Bruce Lane.   In this year's Youth Concerts, the ABC has introduced young people to several famous symphonies. It has succeeded in producing interesting programs, but has also succeeded in ruining them by **playing incongruous encores at every concert**.

A gay Roumanian rhapsody by Enesco was quickly dampened by the "Waltz of the Flowers." As the magnificent "Firebird" finished, we were subjected to the Polovtsian dances from "Prince Igor," a hackneyed piece.   Isn't Stravinsky good enough to finish a concert?

To my horror, after a sensitive performance of Tchaikovsky's tragic "Pathetique," Mackerras forced his pet piece on us – "Pineapple Poll," of course.

These encores have been an insult to the composers whose works have preceded them, and I cannot understand the Youth Concert Committee's bad taste.

Letters, Laurier Williams. I am sure the great majority of people at these concerts thoroughly enjoy the encores, even though they may be incongruous. In any case the mind of youth is flexible and should enjoy such changes in mood rather than criticise them.

I hope that the Youth Concert Committee will continue its policy of allowing encores to be played. They create goodwill and a closer relationship between the orchestra and the audience, and emphasise the informality of the concerts. These surely, are the aims of a Youth Series.

AUGUST NEWS ITEMS

August 4th. Remember **osteopath Dr Ward**, on trial for sordid dealings with call-girls and others in the Profumo affair? After a week on trial, Ward took a massive **overdose of drugs**, and after lingering for four days, **he died**.

Police were reporting that **gangs of rockers**, in **their jeans and leather jackets and driving pre-war hot-rods,** were disrupting dances at places like surf clubs. **Some punch-ups** were inevitable before the police arrive.

Craig Breedlove, in the USA, established **a new land-speed record of 407 miles per hour. Donald Campbell** indicated that he was not deterred and would **return** to "sunny" Australia as soon as Lake Eyre dried out.

NSW illegal bookies were now offering the Government large sums of money to allow them to continue operating, but **now as legal betting shops.** According to their figures, which were certain to be contrived, the NSW Government would be much better off than by using a SP-based system. **Their record for sordidness** would not be easily forgotten in making decisions….

Queensland introduced TAB betting in March, 1962.

The 2-day old son of President and Jacqueline Kennedy died today (August 19th) of a respiratory ailment.

August 8th. Britain's Great Train Robbery was done. "A gang of 20 masked men early today carried out **Britain's biggest most daring train robbery.**" Their haul, in Post Office mail and diamonds, **was over one million Pounds….**

The gang cut telephone and signal wires, and diverted the train to a distant siding. They attacked the driver and fireman with iron bars, and passed the mail bags through the roof of the train to accomplices on a rail bridge. They then escaped in three trucks, leaving the engine crew and mail-sorting staff hand-cuffed together....

August 9th. Britain's banks now estimated that **the loss from the robbery would be three million Pounds. They offered a reward** for 260,000 Pounds for good information.

Five youths, aged from 16 to21, and two instructors of the outward Bound Movement, **were drowned in the Hume Weir** when their canoes were overturned during a sudden rain squall.

August 15th. **Police have arrested three men and a woman** in connection with the Train robbery. They also seized 120,000 Pounds. Then, three days later, three more en and two women were also charged. Loot was found.

Many eyebrows were raised when a Judge **sentenced a man to a lashing** and two years gaol for assaulting his two daughters. This would have been **the first lashing since 1905.** The State Cabinet sat and decided **to remit that part of the sentence**....

Prison authorities were at a loss. They said they did not know what procedure to adopt if the lashings happened. For example, **who should do it?** They also did not know if the Prisons Department **possessed a whip, or would a cat-and-nine-tails be required?**

YOU CAN'T TEACH: YOU'RE COLOUR BLIND

When I was being belted by the nuns in primary school, I had a mate who was a left-hander. He was a good kid and a good student, but the nun took to him often with a 15-inch ruler so that he would **change to writing with his right hand.** In the end, he left the convent school and moved to the Public School, thereby doubtless losing his soul.

But in any case, by the time we come to 1963, there were still taboos that defied any logic. One of these was standing up for the picture of the Queen at the start of picture shows. Woe betide the few rebels who were starting to sit through this. Another was the belief, still held by most Education Departments round the nation, that a person could not manage to teach if he was colour-blind. **Are you colour-blind ? If yes, do not apply for the Teachers' College.**

Equally devastating to the individuals concerned was the attitudes to diabetes.

Letters, Ruby Board, Vice Pres., Diabetic Association of NSW. Some years ago, the New South Wales Public Service Board established a provident fund for the physically handicapped. This enables diabetics to be employed as permanent instead of casual employees on receipt of a certificate from their medical adviser that they are properly stabilised.

The Commonwealth Public Service, on the other hand, refuses to recognise the great strides made by the medical profession in the treatment of diabetes and dismisses immediately anyone found to be diabetic, however suitable they may be for the work.

Thus many desirable employees are prevented from entering the PMG's Department.

There were only two countries, out of the 29, that sent representatives to the last international congress, which did not recognise the improved status of diabetics by admitting them to their Public Service – one of them was Australia!

Letters, J Loudon. I have been refused a permanent position with the service for reasons which I, as a sufferer from diabetes, fail to appreciate. Last October I sought permanency in the department for which I work in a temporary capacity. I submitted to the regular medical examination at the Department of Health, and I was told that I had no chance of being accepted for a permanent post because of my diabetic condition. However, before this was confirmed by a letter from the Public Service Board, I submitted further information to the board in the hope that it would result in a more tolerant hearing of my application.

Encouraged by statements made in Parliament that the Public Service Board would consider qualified handicapped people for permanent appointment in positions for which they were not previously eligible, I made a lengthy submission to the board, enclosing testimonies from the director of the section in which I work, and the doctor from whom I receive treatment.

The director testified that I was able to compete fully on my own merits in the work of the section and that I had sought and been given no special consideration because of my condition. **The doctor said** that my condition was very stable, I had no signs of any complication, my general health was excellent, and that from a medical point of view I was totally fit and my diabetic state should present no difficulty in my obtaining a permanent appointment.

My application was rejected. The board, in the letter informing me of its decision, said that I did not meet the physical requirements set down for entry to the service and it would take no further action on my application.

I have since had correspondence with the Diabetic Association of NSW, which took up my case with the Prime Minister's Department. The association was told that only diabetics amenable to treatment by diet would be considered for permanent positions with the Public Service   All other diabetics are apparently under a complete and lasting ban.

Diabetics are constantly being urged not to consider themselves second-class citizens or employees, yet how can they help but think this when discrimination such as I have outlined exists?

THE NEVER-CHANGING OZ PARLIAMENTS

In the early years after Federation, in the first and second decade of the Twentieth Century, our Federal and State Parliaments established patterns of bad behavior that were **not** the envy of the world. In that period, personal abuse, Aunt Sally questions, false charges, and petty quarrels took precedent over serious matters of State, and thoughtful answers to questions.

By some miracle of social paralysis, we managed to retain that shocking state of affairs through WWI, the Depression, and WWII. But surely, that was enough of that. Surely, when we come to the benign and prosperous years of the early 1960's, our Parliament will not still be practicing the juvenile scrapping of the earlier years.

Let me show you two typical Letters of the period.

Letters, K Doyle. Regardless of their political affiliations, Australians with a proper regard for the dignity and effective function of their Parliaments, will deplore the exhibition of political hooliganism by ALP Members in the House of Reps on Thursday.

I refer to their shameful and disorderly conduct in bringing chaos to the House, and the nation's parliamentary business to a standstill, just because they objected to a statement by Mr Wentworth.

Their rights to object to his claim, that much of the ALP is on the side of our possible Communist enemy, I do not question. But they stand condemned for turning the House into a "bear garden" for two hours, and for forcing its adjournment, merely to protest over this party-political matter.

Letters, C Bale. I, and all Australians, must be ashamed, disgusted and angry with the words and actions of the elected representatives of the people recently in Parliament. Your accounts of their conduct read as if you were reporting a kindergarten's boys brawl.

Have we lost our ability to discuss and fight for our beliefs, whatever they may be, with dignity and a proper regard for decency and order? Or is it possible that we have elected self-centred, small-minded men and women whose vision of their country extends no further that a safe seat and a fat salary.

It would do them good if they could see the light of anger in the eyes of their electors whenever their actions in Parliament are discussed. Have they forgotten that they have a job to do? It is a pity that we have no right to recall a member to his electorate to answer to the men and women who put him in Parliament.

Comment. I think that both of these Letters could equally-well have been written 50years later. You might think that over the course of 100 years, or over 50 years, something would have been learned. But it hasn't. Not at all. So whatever good the Members do **outside** the various Parliamentary sessions, their conduct **inside them** remains farcical.

SOUTH AFRICA'S APARTHEID

After WWII, many nations in the world had wanted to get rid of the colonial overlords, and a lot of these had succeeded. For example, India was about the first cab off the rank, and locally, Indonesia had more recently removed the Dutch. In many parts of the world, especially Africa, various types of foreign domination still held sway over native populations, and were under attack from a variety of different types of movements.

In South Africa, with its large population of Dutch settlers and pioneers from long ago, the fairly recent demands of the native populations for a fair go had moved them to the point of stubborn refusal to budge. It was a difficult situation that was very hard to resolve. The Dutch settlers could rightly claim that they had economically settled the land, and had brought many benefits of civilisation with them. They had set up industries and farms, and had truly settled. What they wanted was to continue this, and to hold on to their superior positions and property and prosperity.

On the other hand, the native populations, the blacks of various colours and tribes, wanted the same resources for themselves. They too wanted security and prosperity and property, and they hoped that by removing foreigners they could get all this.

So the two sides had moved intractably into their positions. The whites had enacted laws that were designed to hold onto their power, and the blacks were now opposing this situation as actively as they could. One part of this was the provision to separate the blacks and whites as far as practical from each other, and it was this policy of apartheid that was now attracting much criticism from the rest of the world.

In Australia, we had our own racial problem with our aborigines, but the agitations – that's all they were – were not bothering the person in the street. As far as South Africa was concerned, most people **here** could read about the oppression there, and say tut-tut, and that was about it. Sometimes, when we were sending Rugby Union teams back and forth, or talking about cricket teams visiting, tempers flared a little, but in our idyllic remote world of 1963, nothing overseas stirred us much at all.

Still, a few writers kept up a small but steady stream of Letters on South Africa. I enclose only one such here, and do not claim that it covers anything like the whole gambit of the subject. It is a purely random, well-written Letter that puts forward just a couple of facets of a very complicated and difficult situation.

Letters, Graham Thomas. Mr Hill believes that a Bantu Government would **massacre the white population** in South Africa, if power were ever to come into their hands. **Very likely this is so,** although there were, and still are, Africans of high education and devoted to the cause of peace who would have worked together with the white man to establish a workable multi-racial society.

Such men are now banned, imprisoned or have fled the country and the leadership of the Africans must, due to the Nationalist policies, fall into the hands of irresponsible, uneducated, hot-headed Africans filled with a hatred and bitterness caused by the inhuman policies, and even more inhuman application of those policies, of the present Government

Not even the amount of sacrifice and devotion by the handful of whites, who are sympathetic to the cause of multi-racialism, can offset the harm that has been done. Whatever the outcome, the white man will only reap the fruit of the seeds he has so willingly and extravagantly sown. Because I do not believe that anything can justify the appalling hardship and cruelty daily inflicted on the African and coloured peoples in South Africa, and because the law does not allow me to oppose it without laying myself open to banning, imprisonment and even death (under the latest law), I have preferred – with all its attendant hardship and heartache – to banish myself voluntarily from South Africa. This was the only protest I and many thousands of South Africans can make, many of us after years of bitter struggle, to alleviate the suffering to which we were daily witness.

While it is perfectly true that there is no easy solution to South Africa's problem, this is no justification for the present state of affairs. There can never be any justification for cruelty, oppression, inhumanity.

BETTING AND THE TAB

In earlier pages, I talked about the NSW Government's interest in getting rid of SP bookies, and introducing a TAB betting system, State-wide. The most common perception of the SP bookies was one of sleaze, of bookies hiding in the back-yard of pubs or lavatories there, or of the same people sitting in cars in front of pubs ready to take off if the Flying Squad raided them. The other side of this was the observation that these SP bookies were notably richer than their patrons, that the local police were always in their pocket, and that they could always find a patsy to take the charges if the Flying Squad got them. In fact, the system, apart from being illegal, was disreputable and corrupt.

As I said, this was the most common perception. Now, with the prospect of a different system that would be seen as completely different, churchmen and politicians and the men-in-the-street welcomed the opportunity to espouse it, so there was a chorus of voices supporting it. Still, as usual, there was another side to it all, and these two correspondents put their case for retaining the old.

Letters, D Brigden. In New South Wales, illegal SP betting has been operating for over half a century and the introduction of a TAB must seem, to many people, rather like nationalising the corner grocery store.

I live in a working-class district where there are many SP punters and I have never heard **any** of these advocate the TAB system. I believe that if a public-opinion poll were conducted among these punters, the vote would be overwhelmingly in favour of one or a number of forms involving SP bookmakers.

One reason for this is that many SP punters would find it difficult, if not impossible, to bet under the TAB system.

At present there are, to my knowledge, three types of SP. betting. These are phone betting, betting shops, and the system of "runners." In the last-mentioned system, an employee of the bookmaker walks a set route before the start of each race, thus enabling punters to bet from their homes. Many of these punters would be unable to walk to a TAB centre), and for many of them the Saturday afternoon racing is their sole means of entertainment.

In addition, many punters in working-class areas bet in amounts as small as sixpence. To these people the introduction of a 2/6 minimum bet will deprive them also of their only entertainment (for, if they cannot afford a 2/6 bet, they cannot afford to buy a TV set, or go to the pictures, the football or even the races).

A further disadvantage of a TAB is that bets must be placed half an hour before the start of the race; because of this, and the general unreliability of tote odds at the start of betting, the "off the course" punter will have only a very poor idea of the prices of the different horses. These prices are an important factor in both the correct selection of a horse and the determination of the size of the wager.

It seems to me that the argument advanced for the TAB by Mr Justice Kinsella and others is equivalent to saying to a man ordering a beer after a hard day's work: "Here, have this tomato juice instead, it's better for you."

Letters, C McCarthy, Racing Commission Agents' Assn., Sydney. You are under no obligation to deal objectively with the question of off-course betting in New South Wales. **The suppression** in Sydney of anything which might tend to make the Government question the wisdom of the Kinsella recommendations, even on such a matter as the cost of its operation, makes it evident that **the Press is quite determined to press for a TAB.** The country Press, on the other hand, regards the matter as one for serious consideration from all angles.

However, how can you deliberately distort the presentation of an alternative, and we believe better plan, which was never considered at the Royal Commission, into a bribe?

There was **no suggestion** that anybody conducting illegal SP bookmaking would automatically be granted a licence, or even considered as an applicant for one. That would be entirely a matter for whatever licensing body the Government may institute.

Naturally, you will not print this letter. That would constitute a breach of the Iron Curtain. Not the political one, but the one set up by **the freedom-loving democratic Press.**

LASHING OF OFFENDERS

In doing my writing, I now have almost 30 books to my credit. I find that every five-or-so years a question that is raised is whether corporal punishment should be used in various ways. It might be as caning in schools, or as lashing for serious offenders, or as solitary confinement and a bread-and water diet for recalcitrant prisoners. Occasionally the question becomes whether hangings can be re-introduced for crimes.

There are always a multitude of arguments both for and against a proposition but, since WWII, I can verify that there has been a revulsion by most of society against measures to revert to earlier days. However, there are times when normal tolerant people are driven **almost** to changing their minds. How often have I heard someone say **"they should hang the bastard"**, and others say **"what they need is the old style police sergeant to give them a bit of rough stuff"**? However, good sense generally prevails, and most people accept the more humane way.

When such controversies erupt, however, there is always quite **a strong contingent** of writers who argue for the tougher measures. This suggests to me that there are, in society, more advocates for tough measures than can be seen on the surface at the moment.

In any case, I will give you just one example of the point-for-point arguments that develop. The aspect they cover is just one of dozens that constantly occur, so I am not trying here to instruct you in those arguments. Rather, I would like you to see that, for anything that can be said, there is an answer. Sensible or otherwise.

Letters, E Speich. On Friday last, Judge Curlewis ordered that a prisoner should receive 10 lashes for a criminal offence upon his own daughter. It has since been stated that the Cabinet of NSW will not permit this punishment to be carried out, as it is "barbaric." Is not **this crime** also "barbaric"?

It has been said that a flogging is degrading. Such a person as this, already degraded, could not possibly be put much lower by being whipped, when such may be the only thing to act as a deterrent, for physical hurt is apparently the only thing understood in this case.

Letters, L Melville. E Speich should get some sort of medal for the complete lack of understanding he displays in his remarks on lashing as a punishment.

The point is not whether this type of punishment degrades the offender; **it degrades society**. The argument that a barbaric crime deserves "barbaric" punishment, if taken to its logical conclusion, would mean that a sexual offence should be punished by having the State perpetrate a sexual assault on the offender.

OTHER MATTERS

Letters, Enid Bell. I have discovered the **new batter-whip all-purpose loaf**! Most people would think it was bread, judging by the size, shape and wrapping. I thought it was at first; now I'm not sure. The wrapper simply mentions this batter-whip business and leaves the customer to discover the exciting possibilities of the matter enclosed. A few minutes' kneading and moulding in one's hand, and lo! No longer is there any resemblance to the staff of life. Odourless, tasteless, colourless!

You can model anything out of it; it is water-repellent and can be submerged for hours without visible change. When walked upon, it adheres firmly to floor surfaces and comes to resemble old chewing-gum. Also, the possums won't eat it. It has a certain resilience and suggests further uses as innersoles for those aching feet.

Letters, J Abbott. It has been announced that the brand name on our butter in the British market is to be "Kangaroo." It is to be hoped that it will not meet the same fate that "Ibis" brand canned fruit is alleged to have met in the East many years ago. When the natives saw the picture of the ibis on the tin they imagined the contents to be tinned ibis, a bird sacred to them. Sales suffered.

Perhaps the more enlightened Britons will think it is kangaroo butter, and maybe they will say how clever the Australians are to train the female kangaroo to let down her milk into her pouch and then hop about until it is churned into butter.

THOUGHTS

The Treasurer, Harold Holt, has relented. The names for our new currency will be dollars and cents. The change of heart was because of the great pressure brought to bear on Members by their constituents.

Letters, Insured. W G McAlister shows himself to be sadly misinformed on the subject of tranquillisers. In the first place, "sleeping pills" are not usually included under the classification of tranquillisers. Tranquillisers are those drugs which induce a calm state of mind without clouding consciousness, reduce tension and agitation without somnolence, and relieve stress and psychomotor activity without depression.

"Sleeping pills," on the other hand, do not have this distinctive action on the sub-cortical tissues of the brain, but have a general depressant action. They belong to the sedative and hypnotic group, which reduce mental activity and induce sleep. These drugs have toxic effects which may be severe in abnormal doses, and can even prove lethal. Deaths have been recorded from the severe respiratory depression caused by the combined effects of barbiturates and alcohol.

Admittedly there is nothing to prevent a would-be addict from doing the rounds of several doctors to collect his doses except that addiction symptoms would inevitably lead to his being discovered.

SEPTEMBER NEWS ITEMS

September 8th, Capetown, **South Africa**. The Australian Wallabies (Rugby Union) team's third and final **Test against South Africa was disrupted for 10 minutes while African rioters and police fought severe battles on and off the field.** The rioters stormed onto the field hurling bottles, and the police responded by charges with truncheons and then by firing revolvers over the head of the surging mess.

The **Amalgamated Engineers Union decided to press for a 35-hour week** in the coal-mining and power generation industries. They claim this is now possible because of the advances made by automation and mechanization. This is the **first reputable Union to seriously make such a claim.** There would be no direct or strike action at this stage.

September 16th. The Malayan Prime Minister today announced the formation of a **new State to be called Malaysia.** It will comprise Malaya, Singapore, Sarawak, and British North Borneo. **Australia supported the union. Indonesia and the Philippines did not**, and recalled their ambassadors….

Sept 17th. In Singapore, the island celebrated with much **glee.** They were finally free from Britain. **In Indonesia, large crowds rioted**, and some of them stormed the British Embassy and burned the Ambassador's car. The next day, 10,000 rioters looted and then set fire to the Embassy itself. The Indonesians were cross because **British North Borneo had been ceded to the new Federation**, and not to Indonesia….

Several correspondents **bemoaned the setting of the sun on the British Empire in the East.** They said that India, and Australia and New Zealand, had long been removed from the British yoke, and that Malaya and Singapore had now broken the chain of command. In fact, **the only British holding, of any worth, in the region was now Hong Kong.** They were distressed that **the pink** that once dominated **the maps of the world**, was now mainly gone, and they thought that probably the **civilising effect** that had come with the pink had gone too.

4,000 members of the public turned out last night at Sydney's Mascot airport **to welcome the new Boeing 727 aircraft. The plane will carry 119 passengers**, and have a range of 3,000 miles, and a speed of 600 miles per hour.

A reprinted 2013 Article in the *SMH* raised the question of whether the **current state of tension between the Arabs and Israel** will **lead to another World War**. It talked about the relatively **minor skirmishes** going on, but asked whether, if they grew to open conflict, other parties would be drawn in and a major conflagration be started....

Comment. Writing now **in 2019**, once again I must wonder that **so little has changed.** Despite the wars and border battles, all the peace proposals and meetings at Camp David, all the Secretary of State bally-hoo, all the bluffs and bravado, all the armaments build-up, **the Article could be used to describe the situation today.**

POLICE UNDER FIRE

Over the last months, the NSW Police Force faced a growing stream of criticism. Its Officers were doing things that made their way into the Press, and reflected badly on them. For example, three separate young men had been shot while trying to escape custody, and several prisoners in detention claimed that they had been bashed by police. Most recently, four clean-cut young men were harassed, and perhaps bashed, at police stations, on a number of occasions, for trying to report the activities of hoodlums.

The normal thing in 1963 in these circumstance, in all States, was for the senior police to put on their serious face, and promise an immediate investigation, and after a few days say that there was no breach of discipline, and that there were no bad eggs in the Force. In most cases, it was possible to believe the first claim, but the second claim was far too sweeping.

In NSW, the *SMH* decided that it was now appropriate to turn attention to the bad incidents of the previous month, and published Editorials on the supposedly bad behavior, and gave front-page space to any incident that questioned the judgement and behaviour of Officers.

As usual, when there is an obvious newspaper blitz, there was a flurry of correspondence. Some of these were from people who just hated the police, and really enjoyed laying the boot in while they had a chance. But dozens of others were a bit more reasoned in their arguments, for and against the Force, and it is these that I publish below.

Letters, K Buckley. It is apparent from my investigations that (a) most of the people who have cause to complain to the Police Department do not do so (they are scared) and (b) when complaints are made to the Department they are generally smothered at a relatively low level by a mixture of soothing words, veiled threats and evasion. I believe that the Commissioner of Police himself is not told about most of these complaints.

It is time that Ministerial responsibility for the police Force was asserted. Equally, there is need for a voluntary civil liberties organisation to take up cases of injustice. Plans are being laid now to form such an organisation.

Letters, E Ellis.   The presence of **armed** servants of the State in our midst, without the presence of armed and violent revolt among the citizenry, is an overt act of belligerence and mistrust towards these citizens. The **policeman with his bulging pistol is taken as the symbol of State coercion,** perhaps subconsciously, and is hated accordingly. The observance of law and order instead of being a civic responsibility becomes an odious obligation.

I wholeheartedly agree with Mr Heffron when he says he is not prepared to stand by and see the police assaulted by people.   But let us be realistic; who would dare to do this and how often?   How many police have been cold-bloodedly slain on duty?   Surely they are aware of dangerous circumstances, and then can bring their weapons either on their persons or in patrol cars for these **particular occasions.**   Let us have an end to this armed effrontery in our midst.

Letters, Anti-Lout.   The prewar conception of the lout has changed – his general habitat was supposed to be in the so-called "depressed suburbs" such as Newtown, Erskineville, Chippendale and nearby areas.

Today, police authorities will tell you that the "centre of gravity" of hooliganism has shifted to young people coming from the so-called better-class suburbs, such as those in the Warringah and North Shore areas.

While not condoning any unprovoked alleged police "bashings," there is only one language that today's vicious, arrogant and pampered larrikin understands – **physical retaliation.** If they invite it, **let them get it back with interest.**

Letters, R Farley. Surely it is ludicrous for allegations made against policemen to be investigated by their own fellow-workers whether they be allegations of brutality, the indiscriminate use of firearms, or even bribery.

Many prominent people, when commenting on such happenings, usually preface their remarks by praising the integrity of the majority of policemen. Is this correct, though? Sometimes the guilty policeman is found out, brought to justice, and punished, invariably because of the action of a member of the public. But **what of the policemen who witness these happenings and do nothing** to report these criminals in uniform, probably because of intimidation or the fear of reprisals? Surely they are just as guilty, and this must apply to many policemen who do nothing wrong by they own actions but condone the wrongdoings of others by their own inaction.

I cannot recollect one instance of a policeman being punished for brutality in which such action was instituted by police officers only, and yet only a knave or a fool would suggest that such improper conduct does not exist among some policemen.

Letters, L Price. When we call on the police to protect us from hoodlums who will not stop when called upon to do so, why shouldn't the police fire on them after they have been warned?

Why arm our police with revolvers if they are not intended to be used? If they didn't use force in some cases, they would be the laughing-stock of every hoodlum that comes to town.

Our Police Force does a mighty job – just think what would happen if we didn't have it.

Letters, B Schumacher. The only way to clear the air over the present bashing disclosures is by an independent public inquiry, with sacking of the Gestapo element, not merely reprimands or demotions.

If this trend continues, the work of the decent policemen will continue to become infinitely harder as public resentment develops into a habit of stony-faced non-cooperation.

No matter how hard the appointed officers try to be impartial in a departmental inquiry, the public will have little faith in their findings; so an open inquiry by Judges is the only way to cleanse the Police Force of the hoodlum element.

Letters, John Playfair. The recent shooting and wounding of an unarmed youth in daylight raises the question of whether it is really necessary for our police to carry firearms. It is a sobering thought that this accident, if such it be, could not have happened in Britain, where police are armed **only with a short wooden truncheon** – both by day and by night.

Letters, Laurence Halloran. So long as we are prepared to accept a Police Force recruited on a brute-strength-and-ignorance basis, we must also be prepared to accept the concomitant excesses. Having regard to the educational standard required of police recruits, and the nominal training considered adequate to equip them for their duties, the wonder is not the number who "go wrong," but rather the number who do not.

What more do we expect? We pay them next to nothing, give them no status, knock them at every opportunity, and then squeal when the force attracts bullies and lurk men.

Here, as elsewhere, the constabulary constitute a social problem, and inevitably so. Anybody who cares to study the daily working of a police station, take in the primitive, barrack-like atmosphere, listen to the talk, observe the comings and goings, note the types, and just think, will at once apprehend the difficulty.

It is superfluous to remark that the general level is not high. Of course it isn't. But if intelligence is not high, "low cunning" is not low; certainly it is sufficient to prevail over the bulk of people with whom the police have dealings. They do not often make the mistake of standing over people who are in a position to defend themselves.

Perhaps the essential point is that within the public at large aggressive mentalities are dispersed, whereas in the Police Force they are united. Who then unites them? More precisely, who acquiesces in an organisation which, by its very nature, must consolidate them in this way? Answer: we do. Yet could the community get along without police? Answer: the community could not. Whether an unavoidable social problem becomes a social menace accordingly is up to nobody else but ourselves.

Letters, Joseph Firth. Could it be that the upsurge of alleged police "bashing" is an indication of police frustration, shared by many thoughtful citizens, at the failure of the notoriously weak Courts of New South Wales to back up police action against hoodlums and thieves.

Repeatedly in the past few years police have worked hard and diligently to bring some vicious criminal to justice, only to see all their work thrown away by some ridiculously inadequate sentence imposed by the Court.

It is time we took another look at our crime rate and our criminals.

Years ago there was some excuse for people who stole, out of desperation, or committed other criminal acts, in an attempt to escape from appalling living conditions.

In these days in this country there is a good living for anyone who is willing to work, and the old "sob story" about the boy who "never had a chance" won't pass scrutiny any longer. The criminal today is a "smart Alec," who thinks that only fools and horses work.

Comment. Apart from these contentious Letters, there were many who pointed out the great job that the police were doing. That they suffered from poor wages, working at all hours, with much criticism from all sides, and some members of the public ever ready to shop them if possible. Other writers asked the question of how we would cope without them, and who does the average citizen call when there is a burglary or assault in the home?

These were perfectly true and valuable comments, and made it clear that most people were on the side of law and order. But the earlier Letters also raised some questions that should have been answered, and problems with rogue officers have remained an issue, albeit a progressively smaller one, over the years.

OZ OVERSEAS TRADE

Things were pretty good in Australia at this time. Lots of jobs, affordable houses being built, tons of barbies, and no pressing national problems. It could be that we were living in a fool's paradise, but as in all such paradises, no one could see it at the moment.

One problem that kept niggling was the suggestion that Britain would join in some form of Common Market with other European nations, and that would spell the end of our nice comfortable trade with Britain. This was important to Oz, and meant big bickies to the producers involved, and to the nation. The countries of Europe had split themselves into an Inner Six, and an Outer Seven so that within each group, favourable tariffs and preferences would apply. Among the welter of proposals being examined, there was one thing that was getting clearer to Australians. That was that Britain would some time, in the near future, start to reduce existing non-competitive trade with Oz.

The man-in-the-street was not worried much by this at all. However, some producers and some corporations, and even some Government Departments and Boards, were very concerned. There was talk about Trade Missions, even to Asia, and there was the current visit to Oz by Japanese Prime Minister, Mr Ikeda, and then more talk about improving our marketing efforts, through Boards, to the world in general.

Again the suggestion that our butter in Britain be labelled as "Kangaroo" raised its head. This dubious piece of marketing **again** met with more derisive comments.

Letters, (Mrs) Jean Dixon.   Referring to and agreeing with J Abbott, it is to be hoped that no edible commodity prepared in this country for export will bear the name "kangaroo."   We Australians, not unnaturally, regard kangaroos with affection, but, after all, we are used to them!   The reaction to this quaint animal by overseas visitors is often little short of revulsion.

A few years ago I escorted the wife of a visiting English businessman to one of our local sanctuaries. It was a hot day, and the kangaroos and wallabies lay about in languid attitudes on the dusty ground. A large number of mother kangas had joeys in their pouches. Not cuddlesome little creatures, but oversized youngsters whose enormous feet protruded quite horribly from the pouch. The view of mother kanga both fore and aft left much to be desired.

My visitor, with an expression of disgust, said vehemently: "I will never be prevailed upon to try kangaroo-tail soup!"

So, if we must use the name "kangaroo" commercially, let us leave it to the transport companies, and find something a little more appetising for our foodstuffs.

Letters, Claude McKay. Like your other correspondents, and as one who supplies a modicum of the milk for butter that could find its way to the British market, I am dismayed to learn that it is to be sold as "Kangaroo Brand."

What makes our butter palatable and health-giving are our sunlit pastures, which contrast, in their favour, with the grey skies of England and the Scandinavian countries. We should be inviting the Brits to savour our sunshine.

We will have koala cheese and wombat dried milk next and so on until we exhaust our fauna. But why "Kangaroo" butter? It is quite conceivable it will be thought to be derived from kangaroo milk.

The average housewife in British cities would have little knowledge of our largest marsupial, otherwise the old "Punch" joke would have had little point. The drawing showed a motherly soul gazing horror-stricken at a kangaroo in the London Zoo where it was described as an Australian native. "Great heavens!" she cried, "my daughter married one of those."

HOLT CAN'T TAKE A TRICK

When our Treasurer, Harold Holt, changed his mind and decided that dollar was a good name for our currency, he might have thought that the whole episode was over. But he would have been wrong. There were more Letters, a few of them supporting him, but many more deriding the choice.

Letters, D Wallace. Dollar is indeed "a rotten name," and it says little for the wisdom of the multitude that clamoured so loudly for it and for the political courage of Mr Holt and his colleagues who so supinely acquiesced that this has been chosen as the new name.

Democracy should not equate with government by the momentary whim of the uninformed. While "royal" may have had overtones of servility to a now-vanished power, surely it was better than this public advertisement of our **willing submission to the North Americans.**

Letters, R Simpson. I wonder why D Wallace is so certain that the adoption of the dollar is a "public advertisement of our willing submission to the North Americans"? Could it not be argued with equal validity that we are thereby **kowtowing to the Chinese of Hong Kong?**

I am a Canadian who, as a boy at school in England, spent much time wrestling with the intricacies of pounds, crowns, half-crowns, florins, shillings and pence (to say nothing of their colloquial equivalents) – and I, for one, heartily welcome the commonsense adoption of the decimal currency, including the opprobrious dollar.

OTHER MATTERS

Letters, B Towns. Instead of waiting until next December to plant the seed thought of "putting Christ into Christmas," why not begin now with the people responsible for producing Christmas cards? So many cards produced as "Christmas" cards have not the slightest suggestion of the true meaning of Christmas.

Letters, Applicant. It is apparently impossible for anybody over 28 years of age to enter the clerical division of the Commonwealth Public Service, unless he is an ex-Serviceman. Those in this category may join up to the age of 50 years and eight months. In all cases the Leaving Certificate or its equivalent is required as a condition of entry.

It is difficult to see why, with the war over for nearly 18 years, the war-service test is still applied as a condition of entry. Is it going to be applied for ever? If not, for how much longer will educationally qualified young men be denied admission, simply because they did not serve in the forces during – or after – the war?

Letters, M Medaris. Three cheers for Stirling Moss. His condemnation of barbecues is fully justified! For uncivilized forms of party-giving, barbecues are an outright winner – even sillier than that modern bacchanale, the cocktail party, with its maudlin, inane chatter!

I have completely barred barbecues in my garden and refuse to accept invitations to these fashionable rituals of charcoal fumes and burnt offerings, meat blackened outside and virtually raw inside (vide Mr Moss), to mention nothing of the next morning's carnage left to the apparently willing host – or hostess to clean up!

Letters, C R Bennett. I think it is time something was done by the Minister for Transport regarding children occupying seats in trains and buses while adults stand. If mothers travelling with offspring, often in the 10 to 12 years of age bracket, haven't enough courtesy to get these kids on their feet, perhaps the Minister could have a loud-speaker system installed on trains, especially during school holidays, asking children not to occupy seats while there are older people standing.

THOUGHTS

The **Sydney Water Board** announced today that it **will re-consider its decision about fluoridation of the water supply**. No details were given. Canberra last week opted for fluoride in its water.

OCTOBER NEWS ITEMS

The movie, **Cleopatra**, was now released in London and New York, and was proving to be **a moderate non-success**. Its main actors, **Richard Burton and Elizabeth Taylor**, were given a pass mark, but its historic accuracy was criticised, and the plot was too complicated. Taylor had 76 changes of costume, and the movie cost $44 million to make. It won four Academy Awards.

The Big Three nations, **Britain, USA and Russia**, announced that they had reached **agreement on banning the explosion of nuclear weapons in space.** This is one agreement that, to the best of my knowledge, all parties have adhered to.

The Lord Mayor of Sydney, Harry Jensen, was encouraging people to be active in Sydney's big Waratah Week Festival. He urged "A **gay week** lies ahead, and I urge all citizens to enjoy themselves." **My, how words can change.**

October 15th. **The cat is among the pigeons**. Prime Minister Menzies announced today **that Federal elections would be held on November 30th.** At the moment, his Lower House majority was only one, and he expected that the (perceived) poor leadership of Arthur Calwell would give him an increased majority. The election would be held one year earlier than necessary. **The next weeks will be hectic for politicians….**

Early comments from political commentators indicate that they are **not certain that Menzies has made the right decision**. Menzies had indicated the points that he **hoped**

the election would be fought on, but it was certain that the Labor Party would attack on other fronts where the Liberals were more vulnerable.

The opening of the Sydney Opera House, now scheduled for 1965, **will probably be delayed a further two years.**

The Nobel Prize for medical science was awarded to Australian Sir John Eccles for his work on nerve cells at the Australian National University. The prize is worth 23,000 Pounds to him and will be presented by King Gustav Adolf of Sweden....

The Caroline Institute in Stockholm **explained** that the prize dealt with "the nerve impulse, an event with a duration of the order of a millisecond and creating a potential of some 100 milli-volts, is the fundamental unit in the code by which nerve cells communicate with each other and carry out commands destined for motor and secretory cells." **Yes .... of course.**

October 27th. **Sir Thomas Playford had been Premier of South Australia for 25 years.** The previous record for a Premier was Sir Henry Parkes, who served for 12 years.

Prime Minister Menzies ordered the re-instatement of a Commonwealth Works Department employee **who was dismissed for not wearing a coat in the Prime Minister's presence.** The man had been working to prepare a reception for the PM in the Commonwealth Offices block, and had later returned to it with his coat off. **The man was restored to his job by Menzies** after his dismissal had been raised in Question-time in Parliament.

AUSSIES UNDER THE MICROSCOPE

When Australians stopped to **look at themselves in 1963**, they rather liked what they saw. Here we were, a prosperous, industrious and happy white nation, not divided by race or nationality, minding our own business, with little class structure, a good standard of education, and all the amenities that modern living could produce. There was no doubt that we collectively had a larrikin streak, that we were a bit rough around the edges, but that was conscious and by choice, and we preferred that image to any other we could compare with. **As someone said about this time, we were indeed a lucky country.**

But some Australians, and many from overseas, saw us a bit differently. They saw what they considered to be our weak-spots and they were happy to report them to us. The following pages pull together some of the Letters of complaints levied against Australians over the year to date. I have not in general included the apologia and explanations proffered by other writers, because that might spoil a good story.

Garbage not disposed of

Over this year there was a constant stream of Letters that talked about the **piles of garbage** that littered all of our public areas. There were broken bottles on the beaches, papers and empty cardboard boxes at picnic areas, meat pies thrust into the mouth-piece of public phones, an apple pie on the face of a statue in Hyde Park in Sydney, confetti in Church grounds, betting tickets thrown on the ground at the races, tram tickets "thrown wilfully into the air", and grey-hound dogs defecating in the streets and also on front lawns, the picking of noses and spitting in public. Aussies had plenty of faults in these areas. Mind you, as many argued, a lot of these would go away if Councils provided rubbish bins in public areas but, as one writer put it, "they spend all their money putting up signs banning the dropping of rubbish on the ground."

Vandalism

This was a popular topic with correspondents. The turning-over of grave-stones in cemeteries, the execution of wheelies on playing fields, the removal of street signs, the painting-over of railway station names, the opening of all windows in a railway carriage on a rainy day, the felling of trees in parks (a popular complaint), and broken phones and smashed phone boxes. These were not considered as adding much to Oz charm.

Vandalism in a big way

The neo-environmentalists among us found that the destruction of old buildings was **vandalism**. Another pressing issue was a proposal to erect a chair lift at Ayers Rock, and this attracted lively correspondence.

Letters, Members of the Spring School, Muloorina, South Australia (list of 94 signatories appended). We have read with alarm and despair of the proposal to erect a chair-lift at Ayers Rock: alarm at the further and wholly unnecessary disfigurement and cheapening of Australia's first natural spectacle; despair at the mentality which approves in any way such panderings to tourism.

The Rock is more than a thing of beauty and a talismanic natural symbol. To the aborigines of the area it is a sacred shrine, the core and heart of the myths which are entwined with their deepest religious beliefs. Surely a nation which would so flagrantly despoil the religious heritage of one of its voiceless minorities would set itself up before the world as philistine, cheap, materialistic and commercial.

Many of the national treasures scattered across the Australian continent have already been disfigured or destroyed. Let us at least protect this, "the biggest single gibber in the world."

Letters, R N Dallimore. What's the difference between private and official vandalism? None, except that the former works in the dark, while the latter acts openly under "authority" and gets away with it. The results are the same.

Can we sit still and take calmly any plan to permit the erection of a chair-lift on Ayers Rock? Only 10 years ago it was necessary to **obtain a special permit to enter the aboriginal reserve** that encloses Ayers Rock, so sacred did we regard this area. But now all hypocrisy is gone, and we openly abuse this sacred emblem while talking big about our desire to help aborigines.

If anyone is too infantile or decrepit to walk up Ayers Rock instead of depending on a chair-lift, let him stay on the ground.

Letters, Ruth Beale. What a charming idea, this is of erecting a chair lift over Ayers Rock – this ancient Bethlehem of Central Australia where the earth mother bore the first Great Initiate, one of the earth's earliest forecasts of the coming of a Saviour.

The rock has been protected hitherto by two specially chosen tribes of aborigines, both gentle, reverent people. Now the somewhat heart-broken aborigines are drawing back and leaving the white vandals in triumph to scrawl their obscure names and steal souvenirs.

But, of course, tourism must be served! I have seen tourists standing on newly made Indian graves at Alert Bay, Alaska, and no arguments would move them – they "wanna make a photograph." Is there any hope or possibility of providing adequate penalties for the destruction or desecration of such places? It would need to be done quickly.

Letter, Tom Baggus. Your recent writers were adamant that they should be allowed to see the world from the top of Ayers Rock, and that a quarter of the population, who are physically incapacitated in some way, should be excluded. If these writers ever went to Europe and saw the benefits of chair lifts in the snow country, they might open their eyes wide enough to see that there are others in the world.

The scarring of Australia's face

Then there is bigger scale vandalism. This Letter speaks for itself. Its origin was Army manoeuvres that involved the destruction a dozen acres of rainforest outback in the Atherton Tableland in North Queensland.

Letters, David Hill. In congratulating Alec Chisholm on his excellent article "The Scarring Of Australia's Face", it would be easy to pronounce the usual platitudes condemning the shocking spectacle, something more is now required.

When a Government allows its Army Department to destroy indiscriminately, by explosives, huge slices of valuable and beautiful natural forests in the course of military experiment, national morality must be at a pitifully low ebb.

Over the past decade I have looked on in horror at the activities of Governments destroying whole islands with "H" bomb tests and polluting the atmosphere in the name of "defence," of scientists being instrumental in attempting to pollute the stratosphere with millions of copper needles in the name of "communications," of our own State Government polluting ocean swimming beaches with sewage in the name of "hospital development," of local municipal councils attempting to deposit garbage into the Harbour in the name of "reclamation."

Would someone enlighten me on just how much people will take before they become really interested in political and civic affairs?

There is, though, another view of the Queensland vandalism.

Letters, A Argent.   Thirdly, all of us regret destroying nature's work, but for Mr Chisholm to imply that the military authorities are bent on destroying the native scene in tropical areas unchecked is quite incorrect. The destruction of a small piece of rain forest at Iron Range is like bewailing the loss of a tuft of grass in a 100-acre paddock. Mr Chisholm should perhaps direct his volleys towards targets nearer home – the Sydney beaches, the Blue Mountains, the Dandenongs.

Finally, unless he is particularly alert, I feel pretty sure that Mr Chisholm would not notice the blast area at Iron Range unless his aircraft flew right over it and then only after it was pointed out to him.

The axe-happy Australia

Along similar lines, and under the above heading in the *SMH,* we are taken to task for another of our failings.

Letters, Geoff Allen. I wholeheartedly endorse the comments by the president of the National Trust of Australia, Mr Justice McClemens, that there is no nation in the world which is so "axe happy" and "bulldozer happy" as Australia.

Undoubtedly progress must come to keep a city alive but is the manner in which so many of our beautiful homes and historic buildings being wrecked to boost the fortunes of a handful of speculators, progress? It certainly would not be tolerated by the authorities in any other country.

Macleay Street, where I live, is rapidly losing its old-world charm at the hands of the wreckers, and few of the beautiful and historic mansions with their charming "Sydney lace" wrought-iron railings now stand.

Future generations will no doubt curse the wreckers of today as in their time there will be nothing of old Sydney, but buildings which will resemble the cigarette packs in a vending machine.

Noise pollution

Probably the biggest offender here was the lawn-mower on a Sunday, though motor bikes and souped-up cars were not far behind. Barking dogs got many a mention, and "Cats, but only in Springtime" were apparently a menace.

In October, the menace to end all menaces was the Mr Whippy Ice Cream cart. These small vans drifted through the towns and suburbs of Oz, selling ice-cream on a cone or between waffles. They came out of hiding on week-ends when kids were at home, and always attracted hordes of customers as they worked their way slowly down the back-streets.

The problem here was that they brought with them their own music, it could be heard for hundreds of yards in every direction. So that, in the middle of Sunday afternoon, when every sensible person wanted a nap, the sound of *Greensleeves* would permeate the air for 15 minutes, and the precious nap would be gone until the same time next week. It was too much for some people to bear.

The subject was stirred up by an edict from Parramatta City Council (within Sydney) that said they would stop the sellers from playing their music.

Letters, L Buckingham. Our public music, other than a few council concerts, used to be merely a seasonal "Silent

Night" or "Jingle Bells" followed by the simpler forms of bell-ringing and yodeling, but recently our friendly ice-cream salesmen have been giving us, entirely free, 10-minute excerpts of English folksongs with motorised percussion, until late evening.

This neighbourhood is now anxiously awaiting a further onslaught of this musical culture, particularly as two eminent councilors have praised it "as serving a useful purpose".

Perhaps some really enterprising vendor could teach us the 1812 Overture (with cannon) at about midnight, or even provide some of the newer concrete music, solely to improve our musical education. One van centrally placed could serve several suburbs.

I personally wish to give three quiet cheers to the Parramatta Council and to those silent services to whom my custom always goes.

Letters, Irate Resident. So Parramatta Council has decided to ban the bell or "tinkling cymbal" from the ice-cream vendor's van of a "quiet" Sunday as well as week days – this to avoid disturbing shift-workers, sick people and others.

It is hoped that the council, having tackled this "ferocious pup," will speedily set out to eliminate the "mastiffs" from the Cumberland Oval and Westmead Speedway on Sundays. From these places thousands of football fans and motor speedway enthusiasts split the atmosphere for a mile around with raucous sounds, disturbing the peace of a Sunday afternoon.

Many patients from the nearby district hospital and private hospitals, as well as residents, have suffered this unholy noise far too long.

Let what is now deemed "sauce for the goose" be "sauce for the gander" also.

Letters, I Gallon. I think the music played by ice-cream vendors is very soothing. One day my wife was having an afternoon rest and she woke up to the sound of "Jingle Bells" being played and said: "How lovely, I thought I was in heaven."

If the question of barking dogs was taken up by councilors in our district it would be more sensible. They just run wild, barking 24 hours a day.

Letters, L Oxborrow. If I Gallon thinks the music from ice-cream vendors is very soothing, he is either nine-tenths deaf or is referring to ice-cream vendors different from those we have in Ryde.

Here they play their infernal music-boxes for hours on end during the day and return to "entertain" us at 9 o'clock at night. We have been spared the agony of blaring transistor radios in public transport, so why can't we be spared from a worse agony where the one blaring tune is played over and over again?

Letters, (Mrs) J Morrell. To the unmusical Australian, any music apart from lawnmowers (preferably before 9 a.m. on a Sunday morning), the screeching of brakes and tyres, impatient honking of horns, and unnecessary revving of engines by "show-offs," is "infernal music". Like fairy-bells in Bedlam, the ice-cream tunes certainly soothe me.

World-image of Australians

Finally, I will end this section with the words of wisdom from a person who doubtless was aware of all the faults I have chronicled.

Letters, Fifth-Generation Australian. One does not need to be a jingoist to agree in toto with Anton Persse-Dottar's letter, "An Insult to Britain". It is gratifying, but not surprising, to learn that foreigners are aware of the widespread influence for good that Great Britain has exercised on the world.

If you really want to know what the world thinks of the "Weird Mob" go east, go north, go west (don't go south, there are only penguins there) and you will find that our brash crudeness, bad manners and overpowering boastfulness make us objects of scorn and derision to black, yellow and white alike.

Comment. I can't let this accusation go unanswered, so I include another letter that seeks to refute him.

Letters, Jim Barnes. The charge was that we were crude, bad mannered and boastful. Let me say to the useless piece of flotsam, (supposedly a Fifth Generation Australian) doubtless with a Pommy accent and with their ingrained capacity for laziness and hatred of baths, that I know more about good manners than any Pom does with their bootlicking and stupid bowing and scraping. Let me add that if I ever come across him, if he ever publishes his real name, I will show him that being a winner in everything and talking about it is not boasting, but just stating the facts.

SHOWING THE FLAG

When the Queen was here, she was well received and the Royal Tour was a great success, and the Oz respect and affection for the Queen were obvious. But that does not mean that rumblings against out ties to Britain were at all rare. In fact, it is obvious to me, summarising the news from year to year, that the mood in this country was swinging against keeping our strong ties to Britain. Part of this came from the realisation, by the ordinary person, that the Brits were about to ditch us in favour of a Common Market. Part of it was that the world around us was rebelling against subservient status, and we too as a nation were looking to sever the intangible ties that bound us to the Mother Country.

In any case, arguments for our complete independence were becoming more public, and more frequent. This little example below demonstrates nicely where the debate was.

Letters, Peter Wood. I noticed on Saturday at the opening by the Prime Minister of the new Commonwealth Centre that two flags waved above the pavement. On the right was the Union Jack, on the left the Australian flag.

Apart from the fact that at the time when Menzies arrived, the Australian flag had sunk inconspicuously into the shadows, I am not sure why the flag of another country should proclaim the opening of a building, however plain, for which each of us has paid in taxes.

I suggest that it might be a better thing in the long run if we were less careful to place the Union Jack in the forefront at public functions. The recent revulsion at the idea of "royal" banknotes shows that, on the whole, we do not favour the self-conscious attachment to England of which some high people make a fetish. This may be a cause for hope rather than shame.

Letters, Expatriate. The English, and I mean the English, and not the British or the Irish, discovered) this land and, so far as I am aware, **apart from a few aborigines, there were no Australians present at the time**.

They also settled it and financed its beginnings, again unaided by a solitary Australian. Still on their own, they proceeded to give the new colony its laws, a political system, and language. Quite a large percentage of the population are consequently of English or British descent. This country is still a member of the British Commonwealth.

Possibly all this could **explain why certain people, as a matter of courtesy, fly the flag of "another country" on occasions.**

NOVEMBER NEWS ITEMS

Things in Vietnam are hotting up. The President and his brother were reported dead today, perhaps by suicide. The US and the Chinese Reds are both interfering and scheming, and it **would not be surprising to see serious conflict** start in the region soon.

Two of **Russia's successful cosmonauts were married** today. One of them was a woman.

Daniel Mannix, Cardinal of the Catholic Church, died on November 6th. The *SMH* described him thus: "He died in the city where he had been the centre of Roman Catholic power for 46 years, and was described at one stage as the **most hated and the most loved man in Australia**." He was famous for a **strict Irish approach** in matters pertaining to the church, **politics** and society.

Australia is to pay 56 Million Pounds for **24 classy US F111 bombers.** Many people said the contract should have been given to a British firm. Others said that since **our defence clearly depends on the US**, then it was quite right that we should have gone with her….

In any case, they were due for delivery in 1965. In fact, a **dozen years later, they still had not been delivered**.

The **visiting South African cricket team** was met at Melbourne airport by about **100 university students** who were protesting against **the Apartheid policy**. They later protested outside the cricketers' hotel. The Victorian Premier, Henry Bolte, at a welcome function later **apologised** for them and said they represented a small minority. **The demo was well organised, and caused no problems....**

The next day, Bolte suggested that the rich region of NSW, the Riverina, **cede to Victoria....**

The NSW Premier, Mr Heffron, responded saying "I am sure the people of the Riverina would no more went to secede than the people of Sydney's North Shore would want **to let him have a loan of the Sydney Harbour Bridge."** For the record, let me point out that the secession did not happen.

A *SMH* article regrets **that fun and adventure have gone from the election hustings.** In the good old days of just a few years ago, election campaigns had their so-called orators all over the nation talking to crowds at public venues, and verbally jousting with the interjectors. **Today,** apart from a few occasions, **all the campaigning is done in front of TV cameras,** with Party leaders solemnly talking about policy promises with as much gravitas as they can muster. The article says that old-fashioned meetings attracted large numbers, but **that no one watches a TV policy speech....**

November 17th. The *Sun Herald* said that the Liberal Party and the Labor Party were **all square in the race to the elections** on November 30th.

Attitudes are slowly changing. **A Japanese full symphony orchestra (with 100 players) will visit Australia next year.**

KENNEDY SHOT DEAD

<u>Dallas, Texas. November 23.</u>   The President of the United States of America, John Kennedy, was mortally wounded by rifle fire in his open car today.

A former US Marine was charged with the murder. He is Lee Harvey Oswald, who has a Russian wife, and is regarded as a Communist sympathiser.

President Kennedy was in a procession driving through large and cheering crowds in Dallas, when he was shot with two bullets. The shots were fired from a five-story building along the route, it was reported.

Mrs Jacqueline Kennedy, his wife, was beside him when the bullets hit, but was not injured. Kennedy died within minutes of being hit by the bullets.

Oswald had been unfavourably dismissed from the Marines, and had vowed to get revenge. The police are apparently convinced that he was the sole assassin.

<u>News Item, Washington, November 24.</u> The funeral of President Kennedy will be held in a few days' time. Condolences from all over the world have poured in, and the leaders of most major countries of the world will attend his funeral.

Reaction of the public both in America and elsewhere has been one of shock and horror.

News item, Sydney, November 24. The Prime Minister, Mr Menzies, and the Leader of the opposition, Mr Calwell, have both announced that, because of the looming elections, they **reluctantly will not attend the funeral.** They will both send high-ranking deputies.

OZ REACTION TO THE ASSASSINATION

Personal comment. On that day, very early Saturday morning, I happened to be on a double-decker bus with a male friend, going through the Rocks area in Sydney. We looked out the windows and saw a paper-boy with a banner that screamed **"KENNEDY SHOT DEAD."** We both turned to each other, and in a masterpiece of Australian understatement, both said "Struth" at the same time, and then lapsed into silence for a few minutes. In fact, there was not much more to be said. The deed was done, it was a terrible loss to the world, and no amount of talking would make any difference.

Over the next few days, most of Australia reacted the same way. For once, we forgot our brazen proclivity to over-talk, we dropped our cynicism towards almost everything, and genuinely grieved and wondered about what sense there was in the world. Kennedy was seen by Australians as the one politician who had an ounce of common sense, and as one who might just rise above politics to achieve some permanent good in the world. He was seen to be head and shoulders above any politician we had in this country, and in any other part of the globe. I add that, in writing these books I have talked to hundreds and hundreds of people, and not a single person has forgotten that day, they all remember where they were when they heard the news, and not one of them had anything bad to say about the President.

LETTERS ABOUT THE ASSASSINATION

Communist involvement. The first Letter published in the *SMH* was from the spokesman for the Communist Party in Oz. He obviously wanted to distance his Party from the Press coverage that said that Oswald was a fellow-traveler of the Reds. In fact, that turned out to be **a journalistic red-herring**, designed to whip up anti-Red feeling. However, the idea had no legs and no reputable persons continued to push that line.

Letters, L Aarons, Vice-Chairman, Communist Party of Australia, Sydney. The Communist Party of Australia regards the assassination of President Kennedy of the United States as an example of senseless individual terrorism to which Communists have always been firmly opposed.

A man now charged as President Kennedy's assassin has been described as a "Communist supporter." But such an action as this has nothing in common with the Communist movement.

There is great danger to the world in using this occasion to sharpen international tension.

We join in the world-wide expressions of sympathy to President Kennedy's widow and family and to the American people who elected him to the highest office in their country.

Such words were of no avail with the anti-Communists in Oz society. **They persisted with their propaganda**, and tried to extract as much mileage as possible from the situation.

Letters, W Haraszti-Hart. Mr L Aarons' letter must not remain unchallenged in the face of our (not his) world's loss of the man who knew and spoke the only language the Communists understood, namely that of strength and firmness.

No double-faced, cynical acting of mourning from the Communists can bring Mr Kennedy back to life and leadership of our world. Indeed, he may well be irreplaceable.

As for this not being their way or not having anything in common with their movement, we may again look at facts instead of cynical actors, and we will find that people have been and are dragged from their homes, deported without trial, shot, tortured, kidnapped, etc., for beliefs different from theirs.

To put the lie to Mr Aarons and his comrades we all may look at their own ranks and find that, for example, Trotsky died of assassination by Communists after years of hiding from them. More recently Imre Nagy, Premier of Hungary, has been arrested and finally murdered in spite of promised safe conduct. These and all other known facts should prove sufficiently whether the murdering of such a fine man has anything in common with the Communist movement.

They should not be allowed to express sympathy for something they surely welcome as a heavy blow to the free world.

Lack of musical tributes. Some people thought that there were not enough displays of grief from the rest of the population. For example, the radio and TV stations were criticised for not making greater adjustments to their programs.

Letters, K Kwok. It is most regrettable to see the absence of much respect shown in Australia towards the death of President Kennedy, even though "we in this country had a friend in the late President." While the Russian radio cancelled its normal program and played solemn music, none of the radio stations here, not even the ABC, made any such changes and followed the announcement of the assassination with "pop" music.

I would be ashamed were I Australian.

Letters, T Barnett. I feel I must utter a protest at the almost casual public attitude in this country towards the momentous and tragic happening in America on Saturday.

Was this really just another big news event? Did no Australian realise that such an event, depending on its origin, could set off a world holocaust, as actually happened not so long ago?

Furthermore, surely in that hour of agony for our erstwhile rescuers (from invasion) and our most influential ally, an act of respect through a temporary break in our more noisy and frivolous activities could have been expected from us?

Yet Saturday's shopping spree, the rush to the beaches and elsewhere, the orgy of gambling, drinking and frolicking all went on as usual, to the accompaniment of the usual stream from radio and TV stations of light music, films, plays, shows, etc., many of American origin, be it noted.

Have we become morons, unmoved by great events that do not actually tear the skin off our own backs? Or perhaps our friends across the Pacific have become less important to us these days? If this is the case, we had all better learn to speak Japanese and Chinese – and quickly.

The radio and TV stations replied with dignity, and many of them pointed out that they had adjusted their programs greatly, though not to the same extent as in some other countries. As one radio station put it, "there is only so much dolorous music you can play before people turn off. In any case, people have to continue with their lives, and that does not mean that they are not deeply sympathetic. If we got the balance wrong for some people, we also know we got it right for most of them."

Our politicians did not go. The Party leaders faced a difficult choice. The death of Kennedy was a tragic event involving one of our closest friends. There were politicians from other countries, many of whom despised the aspirations of Kennedy, who were going. Surely, Menzies and Calwell should pack up immediately.

Yet, there was a belief that the elections in Australia were important too, and that the leaders should stay with them till the end. Often they went overseas to assemblies and came away with nothing to show for their efforts. In these circumstances, it was **certain** that nothing tangible would be achieved.

So neither of them went. There were some critical Letters about this.

Letters, J Green, D Brennan, A de Vos. Australia as a nation has treated the assassination of President Kennedy with uncalled-for callousness.

First, this tragic occasion demanded that no lesser person than our Prime Minister should pay this nation's last respects to an honoured friend. **Secondly** the Leader of the Opposition would have won many admirers by electing to go also. But no, this was not to be. A senator, no doubt able, but nevertheless almost unknown to the average Australian, and a complete stranger to the American nation, was chosen to go.

Admittedly, Australia is in the throes of a general election, but surely replacements could have been made in respect of personal appearances to have enabled the two party leaders to attend the funeral of the late President.

Letters, (Mrs) J Walker. Party politics in this country have sunk to a new low. Why did not the Prime Minister and the Leader of the Opposition charter a fast airliner or order an RAAF flight to the United States and together attend the funeral of President Kennedy?

This action would have damaged no party's prospects in the coming election and would have been effective in satisfying the desire of the Australian people to pay the best possible tribute to the slain President of the country whose friendship is so vital to us.

Not everyone agreed.

Letters, Dorothy Seldon. I cannot agree with your T Barnett that the Australian attitude over President Kennedy's assassination is casual.

All those with whom I have come in contact are deeply shocked and personally grieved by the tragedy, but in a situation such as this, the man in the street must be given direction. Australians are loyal and trusty friends and do not forget the debt they owe their American allies.

Had a day of mourning been decreed on Saturday by leaders of this nation then the people would have willingly and thankfully responded.

Letters, M Lyne. How petty are those who criticised Sir Robert Menzies for not attending President Kennedy's funeral.

Most people will agree that first and foremost Sir Robert is a patriot. He implicitly believes that a Government win at the election is vital to the future of Australia. Indeed the life of the country may well be at stake. Should he be condemned for putting his country first?

Rather than lose votes as has been suggested, he is more likely to gain them by his patriotic action in remaining in the country at such a crucial time in the country's history.

Letters, (Mrs) H W McNary. As an American of almost five years' residence in Sydney, I feel that I must point out to Mr T Barnett that both my husband and I have had a different impression of the Australian reaction to the assassination of President Kennedy.

We have been approached on every hand by friends, colleagues, acquaintances . . . even strangers recognising our accents. These sobered and concerned people have touched us deeply by their awareness of and involvement in our great national tragedy.

Letters, J Bingham, Eastwood. T A Barnett cannot be as sensitive to public feeling as he claims to be, else he would have sensed the shock that the assassination of President Kennedy caused the average Australian.

In households everywhere, as the news was received, a sense of personal loss was felt and the sympathy for Mrs Kennedy and her children was profound.

In churches throughout the land on Sunday last as one joined in prayers and stood in silence in memory of a great leader of a great ally, one would indeed have been a moron to be unmoved. Many an Australian tear was shed then and in the privacy of homes also.

THE FEDERAL ELECTIONS

These were all set for Saturday, November 30th. The Liberals (with their much smaller coalition partner, the Country Party) and Labor were slugging it out neck and neck according to the polls. Both were making promises that they could never hope to fulfill, and both were slinging as much mud at their opponents as they could muster.

The people of Australia were not at all excited by the election. They recognised that the Liberals, who had been in power for a dozen years, had lost all their crusading zeal and were now bent on scraping through to the next election. Labor, with the albatross of Communism wrongly tied round its neck, was neither here nor there. In its social programs, it seemed to be a mile behind the Libs most of the time, and responded with "we'll do that too, only better." Both Parties seemed to be thrashing round looking for real issues, and looked incapable of finding them.

They **did** differ on American bases in Australia, and on the deployment of Australian troops to keep the peace in Malaysia. But Labor's insistence, that it had different policies, was too remote for the average voter who, it must be said, was about as insular as you could be in a well-educated society. So, ideology was out the window and, like most Oz elections, the hip-pocket vote would be the winner. It was pretty clear that if the Government **did** change, there would scarcely be a ripple after the first mad period of heightened oratory that can always be expected from a new government.

Comment. For as long as I can remember, the Australian press has over-worked the word "apathetic". Here, though, I must use it again. The public seemed apathetic. It seems that everything was alright, mate, and she'll be right in the future. Anyone might have thought that an election would have brought forth all the fiery rhetoric that it had in the past, all the wonderful and stupid suggestions of what could be done, and all the ratbags pushing their idiosyncrasies. But this time, nothing. Well, nothing much. I give you below the best two *SMH* samples of the campaign.

Letters, F Shepherd. The Prime Minister in his policy speech announced a scheme to aid young people to acquire their own homes. The conception was no doubt sincere, but the practical implementation of the idea is not as generous as the Prime Minister might imagine.

He gave as an example the young couple who saved 750 Pounds. They would receive 250 Pounds from the

Government. I am a mechanic by trade, married with three children and under 35, and I can assure the Prime Minister that with present living costs I have as much chance of saving a substantial deposit over three years for a home as I have of being an astronaut.

What is required is a system of low deposit home purchasing – 100 to 250 Pounds – with reasonable interest rates and repayments over an extended period. Young people have a lifetime to pay off the house and with the security of the property there is little risk to the lending authority.

The Government's scheme will only help those in the higher income brackets.

Letters, Lionel Earl. As a middle-aged citizen with a wife and four children, I have been trying for years to save sufficient deposit to purchase a home.

I listened with interest to the Prime Minister's policy speech and was dismayed when I heard him announce that free gifts of money were to be given to those "under 35" in proportion to the sum they had been able to accumulate.

I have nothing against the youngsters receiving this assistance, but I think it is a poor state of affairs when I and those of my "medium vintage" are singled out for discrimination of this nature.

You might see what I mean. These are two, good, sensible Letters, putting their case for some sensible policies. What I was looking for were some fiery epistles on socialism, the Chinese so-called threat, State aid for schools, the need for women jurors, the lack of discipline among the scrubbers, the lack of religion in Government, and the like. But I got none of these. What I got was two perfectly logical Letters about housing problems. That, my friends, was not good enough. I want my money back. .

DECEMBER NEWS ITEMS

The NSW Cabinet has fixed **July 1ˢᵗ next as the date for the start of off-course betting.** A desperate last-minute effort by SP bookies to have a parallel system, with themselves licensed, was defeated. So TABs will start in NSW from that date. Most other States already have the Tab, or it was on the way.

Post Script fifty years later. The industry is changing again with the proliferation of **on-line betting**. Why travel to the TAB when you can do your betting **on-line**? **Lose your money in the comfort of home.**

NSW primary schools will start **teaching the intricacies of decimal currency from next year.** Tuition will include games with counterfeit money to give practice in handling coins and change.

December 9ᵗʰ. The son of Frank Sinatra was abducted at gun-point from a motel on Lake Tahoe in California. It was known that the kidnapper and victim crossed over into Nevada, so **the FBI was called in**. Frank Sinatra flew in, leaving the set of a movie he was starring in. The movie was *"Robin and the Seven Hoods"*. **Dec 11ᵗʰ. Young Frank Sinatra was released by his captors after 240,000 dollars were paid** by his family as ransom. The kidnappers had talked on the phone to Frank Senior. The young man was hungry, but unharmed….

Dec 15ᵗʰ. The FBI arrested three men in connection with the Sinatra kidnapping. The **240,000 Dollar ransom was recovered in full.**

During summer months, **Roman Catholic clergy in the Bathurst** (NSW) **Diocese** "may dispense with the Roman collar, and **wear an open-neck white shirt**." The dress is optional, and may be worn from November 1st to April 30th. It is understood that it is the first time Roman Catholic clergy in NSW have been permitted to dispense with the traditional collar.

Parramatta Council stuck its neck out again, and tried to stifle the **noise of church-bells in its shire**. Letters started again, and quickly condemned cars and buses, motor bikes with mufflers, motor bikes without mufflers, and all aircraft in and out of Sydney. Then, back to nature, cicadas, crickets, and cricketers. Finally, one writer complained about the noise from his pet **gold-fish** sloshing about in a tank. The Editor then closed the correspondence.

Bogle and Chandler was still not solved by 2019. Theories changed over the years, but the whole episode remains a mystery. The latest theory is that it was caused by **marsh gas**, a form of methane that might be generated by rotting material in the stream. Even if that is assumed to be the cause, **there is still a lot of explaining to do**.

At the end of the year, the Brits were still talking about joining the Common Market, **the Great Powers** were still talking about a freeze on nuclear weapons, the **US and Russia with China** were at the same time building up to the Vietnam War, and this country was still enjoying a **few good strikes** every week. All of this steady activity could be relied upon to go on, and on, and so it gave **a feeling of stability and security to the ordinary life**.

BACK TO REALITY.   ELECTION RESULTS

The result: the Libs retained control of Parliament, and won by more than 20 seats. A bit of a surprise, huh?

Picking over the bones: my comment. The post-mortems on Labor's poor showing started on December 1st, and lasted for the full month. My own view is that the Labor Party could never win an election with Calwell as leader. I would like to offer three arguments to support that statement.

Firstly, the public could not accept that Labor policy should be directed by **the 36 Faceless Men**. The idea that the Party Leader and his Deputy – who had been elected by the people – should have their every move dictated by these un-elected dinosaurs from the States and the Unions, was contrary to our ideas of democracy. Until Calwell stood up to these men and forced a change, he could gain no swell in popular support.

Secondly, Menzies always played on fears of Communism. Calwell had in his Caucus, and in his backing from the Labor movement, many officials who were at least fellow-travellers with the Reds.

Thirdly, and this ties in with my second point above, it was obvious that Calwell wanted to socialise the nation. It was clear that the nation did not want to be socialised. But Calwell would never say clearly just what it was that he wanted to socialise, and how far his socialisation would go. Voters were quite ready to accept, and pay for social security payments, and to accept some level of Commonwealth control of health services and payments. But would he also want to socialise the banks? What about the coal industry, as in Britain? And the steel industry, also in Britain? He would never make a definite statement, and strong doubts were left in the minds of the electorate.

Having said that, my opinion is only one of many. So, I will give you a few others.

Letters, David Glass. I feel I must comment on Mr Calwell's review of Labor's election defeat.

I am 23, getting married next year, and this was my first Federal election. From my own observations, it seems that one of the main reasons for Labor's defeat was its failure to gain the vote of the under 30s.

I wholeheartedly agree with Mr Calwell's attack on tactics used against the ALP. Also I saw the DLP ads on TV, and read **the advertisements exploiting the threat of Communism in the ALP**, which Mr Calwell called "disgraceful" and "disgusting." But I did not once hear, see or read Mr Calwell or any of his colleagues get up and publicly deny these allegations, or at least state the exact relationship between the ALP and the Communists.

I realise that I still have a lot to learn about politics, but I am sure that if this had been done it would have cleared up a big question mark in a lot of young people's minds.

Letters, Lew Payne. Before the elections are buried, could we have a little brutal truth – just once?

Australia will not accept Mr Calwell as Prime Minister and head of a Federal Government at any time, or under any circumstances, simply because **it just doesn't like the look or the sound of him for the part.** If, in fact, Mr Calwell has excellent qualities he must look as if he possesses them. If Labor, at any time, has a good policy and a good team to apply it, then its leader will have to **look** the personification of these things, and he must be chosen for that specific capacity. Sir Robert Menzies qualifies by just 200 per cent. He not only is a suitable photogenic figurehead, he **is** the whole team.

The ebb and flow of voting expresses nothing except the degree of exasperation of the electors with Sir Robert Menzies at any given moment. With me, exasperation is at a permanent summit. I just hope that I live longer than Sir Robert does, and that the country's windpipe proves tougher than his fingers.

Letters, H Kahana. The party which wins elections is the party which is attuned to the popular sentiments of the time. The Liberals, ever alert, do not waste any time when they are convinced that the popular mood is changing. They are more flexible and less rigid in their attitudes than are their Labor opponents.

Labor should not be too proud to learn from the Liberals. If Labor will attempt to tailor its policy to the conditions of the times and not try to make the times fit its policy, then the ALP may win elections, DLP or no DLP. Somehow the ALP policymakers must learn to observe the popular mood and act accordingly. Perhaps younger leadership may achieve this.

Mr Calwell put up a valiant fight with the rather vague material he had to work with. The ALP policymakers will need to supply him with much sterner stuff than this if elections are to be won. If the electorate is worried about foreign affairs, a good policy on education is not election-winning material.

Letters, B Baker. Patricia Cameron may be infuriated by the "Herald" but let me hasten to assure her that this infuriation is typical of the frustrations of the doctrinaire eggheads who make up a portion of the Labor Party's followers.

Year in year out, they give vent to their bigoted class-war ideas only to be ignominiously defeated at each election. Personally I hope the Labor Party does come out in favour of socialisation – it will consign them to the political wilderness for a further 20 years.

To speak of socialism as the only just and rational form of government and inevitable anyway is absolute nonsense. It betrays a way of thinking that became extinct a decade ago. It is the very thing that helped lose the election for the Labor Party.

The Australian people are prosperous and maturing rapidly in a political sense. They have no brief for a party composed of bitter inept theorists, who, while having no foreign policy, try to buy their way into power every three years with a series of promises to everybody.

The Labor Party is the reactionary party of today.

CHRISTMAS IS HERE AGAIN

Every year at about this time, Christmas seems to bob up. This year, as is usual, this special occasion of goodwill to all men was marked by a welter of Letters that grizzled and complained about most aspects of this wonderful festive occasion. Usually, I get my Christmas kicks by publishing all the most abusive Letters, and ignoring the others. This year, just for fun I have graded a few of them, and started with the nicest one I could find, and moved through to a truly jaundiced message of ill-will towards all.

Letters, E Legg. Someone has aptly described the average Christmas drinking party as an occasion where one says the same sort of thing to the same sort of people one sees just about every day of the week, only one says it louder.

That is one side of the Christmas spirit which vanishes almost as quickly as the spirits which are consumed. How about the other unsung side, which is remembered with gratitude for a long time after the festivities are over. To give a couple of instances which came my way recently – the usherette in a city theatre who gave service with a smile and advised me how to change my seat for a better one; and the plumber who did a small job of work and refused remuneration, saying, "Pay me next time."

Letters, Ron Lockerbic. News today that the Post Office has had fewer than ever letters from children to Santa Claus should give most people reason to think hard.

My idea is that the Post Office print a suitable card and send it to all the children who write in to Santa, acknowledging their efforts. What a genuine thrill this would be!

I doubt any taxpayers would object to this, and if extra staff can be organised to handle Christmas mail and parcels which are not half as important, surely this little and unselfish effort can be dealt with similarly.

As man grows older and more sophisticated, let us not lose one of the finest treasures of life – a child's illusions.

Letters, Bruce Ashby. I do not want any presents, or Christmas cards, or Christmas cake, or plum pudding, or nicey-nicey greetings. Don't bother with your "Merry Christmas" and church bells and stupid overseas songs about snow and reindeer. I do not want bucolic clergymen talking about some fictitious bloke who was not born of man, and who came back to life. I can get that type of stuff from Buck Rodgers comics. I want the pubs to be open, the shops to be open, newspapers to be a decent size, and not full of sickening goodwill. Just leave me alone, and mind your own business.

SUMMING UP 1963

If someone told you that the year started with the Bogle-Chandler deaths, and finished with the death of Kennedy, you might get the impression that the whole year was full of sensation. In fact, it was quite the opposite. Apart from a few hiccups, it was a steady-as-she-goes year. Granted there were a few matter that got people stirred up. Like fluoridation, schoolchildren in the sun, and bringing in the TAB.

But these were minor in the scheme of things. For the most part, for most of the work-ready population, for most families and singles, the background news was benign, not much impacting on their daily lives, and left people free to get on with their own activities. Let me just say that economic and work conditions were pretty good, political conditions were much as you might expect, and social activity was fun-filled and light-hearted. There were still annoyances like the housing shortage, and bad roads, and noisy fish in tanks, but there were plenty of barbies so you could grizzle freely about these things.

Last year, 1962, I said much the same thing, and I suggested that readers, born in that year, should **celebrate their luck** by giving their loved one a big hug. It seems to me that this would be a good strategy for this year too, and **I will wait while you do this.**

A small diversion: a glance at the future. Comparing this year with 1962, I thought I saw some trends getting quite a bit stronger than they were last year, and I might ask you to keep an eye on **four** of these.

Firstly, there was the trouble being stirred up in Vietnam. The big guys, America and China, and Russia, were making a mess of things there, and political and military happenings did not bode well for the future. We all know that the situation **did** boil over, and all four nations got involved in a great war of destruction and many deaths. We all know that Australia came in on America's side. We did not know about the war at the time, but it was getting more obvious that real trouble was in the air, and that the idyllic conditions of 1963 could well be challenged soon.

Secondly, there were increasing demands for equality for aborigines and for women. For **aborigines,** events overseas, in places like South Africa and America, were pushing race issues onto the front-page every day. More and more white people were starting, slowly, to see the similarities that applied equally well to Oz, and were starting to talk about it. This movement had a long way to go, but it had started.

Women were becoming more vocal, and were getting a lot of support from men. It was a bit early for the great emancipator of women, the pill, to enter the scene, but there was clearly a greater voice for women than previously.

Thirdly, we were drifting away from our links to Britain, and perhaps replacing them with ties to the US. As for **Britain**, anyone with a brain could see that the Brits sometime soon would join some form of European market, and we would need to find other trading partners. As for **America**, we were giving it bases on our shores, and entering into military agreements, and buying high-speed bombers from her. We were accepting too, American influences, like movies, music, clothing, slang, hatred of Reds, and so on, whether some of us liked it or not.

Fourthly, there was a gradual acceptance of our position within Asia, and the folly of our White Australia Policy. Our links with Japan had grown throughout 1963, and it seemed that, some day, we would accept them for what they are, just people, like us. But resentment of their war-time atrocities was still deep among many people, and that day still seemed a long way off.

Back to my main theme. 1963 was a good year for most Australians. If every year was as good as that, we would be blessed. But, come to think of it, **most of our years since then have been that good.** In any case, 1963 was a good year to start living in this lucky and wealthy country so most infants got off to a great start.

If you were born in that year, I congratulate you on your choice. I trust that all your decisions since then have been as astute and, in any case, that you have worked out for yourself a way of life that is comfortable, and filled with contentment. I add that if by chance your contentment is spoilt by the noise of goldfish in the middle of the night, then Beethoven's Ninth, played full bore, completely covers up their noise, and you are then free to go back to the land of contented dreams.

Chrissi and birthday books for Mum and Dad and Gran and Pop and Aunt and Uncle and cousins and family and friends and work and everyone else.

Don't forget a good read and chuckle for yourself.

At boombooks.biz